To Alan and David, my couple of Champions

To Jerry

all good wishes

for your

Birth Day

August, 2nd

1977

from

Da +

Nang

Regency & Rogue

First published 1976
The O'Brien Press
11 Clare Street Dublin 2.
ISBN 0 905140 06 0

Cover Design Jarlath Hayes

Layout and Design Michael O'Brien

Printed by E. & T. O'Brien Ltd.
11 Clare Street, Dublin 2.

Binding John F. Newman

Typesetting Redsetter Limited

Regency Rogue

Dan Donnelly
his life and legends

Patrick Myler

O'BRIEN

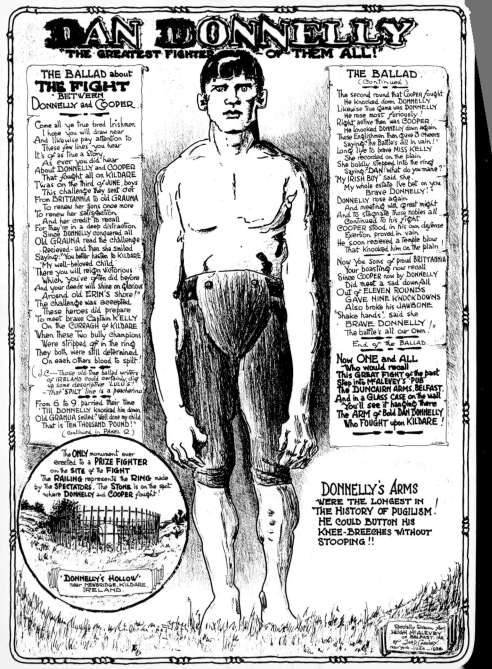

Contents

Left — The sketch on the wall of The Hideout, Kilcullen, claims that Donnelly's arms were the longest in the history of pugilism. It was drawn by Joseph P. Carney of New York in 1934 for display in the Duncairn Arms, Belfast.

LIST OF ILLUSTRATIONS page

Foreword

Heavyweight boxing champions have always been the world's heroes. Ask almost any schoolboy what he would most like to be when he grows up and the odds are he will answer: 'Heavyweight champion of the world'. A recent survey showed that the best known man throughout the world today is not President Ford, Pope Paul or John Wayne — but Muhammad Ali.

For all its basic brutality, there is a glamour, an excitement, a chilling charisma about 'the big fight' that few other staged events can match.

Dan Donnelly, the subject of this book, does not rank among the greatest boxers of all time. But no other man who ever stepped into a roped square to test his strength and courage against an opponent is so well feted in story, in legend or in song.

The idol of the Irish poor at a time when they needed a champion, he was equally at home in the company of the nobility who sought his companionship at the height of his fame.

Those who have written about him over the century and a half since his much-lamented sudden death have almost invariably cast him as the archetypal Irishman. Devil-may-care, good humoured, with a roving eye and a fatal fondness for whiskey and 'porter'.

In researching this book, the first biography on Donnelly since an over-patronising attempt by T. G. Hazard shortly after the boxer's death in 1820, one of my great difficulties has been separating the facts from the fantasy. In attempting an honest appraisal of his life and times, I may have succeeded — if that is the right word — in exposing some of the popular legends as either generously embellished or outright fallacy. Where there is no proof for or against a story, I have given the accounts as I found them.

What cannot be denied is Dan Donnelly's right to his place in the history of his period. That he stands out as a personality in the Regency era, an epoch noted for its outstanding — and often outlandish — 'characters' says much for his impact on the Irish and English scene.

I found it surprising that no genuine attempt had been made to chronicle the life of this remarkable man. I hope I have managed to redress the unpardonable oversight.

Patrick Myler

ACKNOWLEDGEMENTS

The author hereby expresses his sincere thanks to the many people who helped, advised and encouraged him in the researching and writing of this book. He is particularly indebted to the reading room staff of the National Library of Ireland, whose courtesy and unfailing assistance served in no small way to lighten his task.

He is grateful to Mr. Dara O Lochlainn for permission to reproduce the music and words of 'Donnelly and Cooper' from his late father's book, *Irish Street Ballads,* to William Heinmann Ltd. for permission to quote from *The Prince of Pleasure and his Regency 1811-1820* by J. B. Priestley, to Mrs. Alice Little for permission to use an extract from her late husband's book, *Malachi Horan Remembers,* and to Liam C. Martin for permission to use two drawings which first appeared in the 'Know Your Dublin' series by J. B. Malone in the *Evening Herald.*

Thanks also to James J. Byrne, junior, of The Hideout, Kilcullen, Michael J. Tutty, of the Old Dublin Society, Capt. C. Costello, of the Kildare Archaeological Society, J. B. Lyons, librarian, Royal College of Surgeons, Dublin, Graham Houston, editor of *Boxing News,* Senan Carroll, news editor of the *Leinster Leader,* and to the library staffs at Trinity College Dublin and Pearse Street, Dublin.

A special word of gratitude to those who helped in one way or another: Patrick F. Byrne, Thomas Myler, P. J. McCall, P. J. Prendergast, Henry B. Fottrell, Bernie Small, Michael F. Gill, Gilbert Odd, John Murray, James N. Healy, Pat Walsh and the Chief Herald, Genealogical Office, Dublin Castle.

The Office of Public Works kindly gave him permission to visit the Royal Hospital (Bully's Acre) graveyard at Kilmainham, Dublin, and Muriel Gardner helped type the final draft.

Finally, thanks to the publisher Michael O'Brien and his wife, Valerie, for their co-operation.

In the depths of night, by the light of an oil lamp, the body snatchers struck. They sold the corpses to the anatomy schools, which were forced to engage in the grisly trade because the supply of bodies from legitimate sources was inadequate.

A COLD, CLINGING mist blanketed Dublin early on the morning of February 21, 1820. It provided suitable cover for the two burly young men as they dug feverishly at the frost-hardened earth in the graveyard next to the Royal Hospital at Kilmainham.

Despite the severity of the weather, the sweat soaked the shirts of the grave robbers. But there was no time to pause for a rest. They knew only too well that if they were observed at their nefarious act they would be made pay for their sins — probably by being hanged from the nearest tree.

After what seemed an eternity, one of the men's spades struck its objective. The two villians exchanged a quick grin of satisfaction as they hurriedly scooped the wet soil from the top of the coffin.

So far, so good. No one had heard or spotted them. They smashed open the lid of the coffin and unceremoniously removed the corpse. They dumped it into a sack and tied the open end. An accomplice, who had been acting as look-out, gave the all-clear. The prize catch was hoisted over the graveyard wall and hidden under a pile of rags on a horse-drawn cart.

The bodysnatchers, chuckling with satisfaction at the ease with which they had performed their grisly job, climbed aboard the waiting vehicle and disappeared softly into the fog.

Well might they have been satisfied with their morning's work. If the various schools of anatomy in Ireland and Britain were so desperate for bodies that they would willingly pay £10 or more for a recently-interred corpse, then this one, with its perfectly developed muscular structure, must be worth twice the normal amount.

For the bulky sack that now tossed about as the horse and cart beat a hasty trail along the bumpy roads towards the city contained the remains of none other than 'Sir' Dan Donnelly, the pugilistic hero of Ireland.

The report of the body-snatching hit the public, already in deep mourning after the sudden death of the Irish heavy-weight champion at the age of 32, with the impact of a bombshell.

Who would have dared to do such a thing? Their much-loved champion, he who had never met his conqueror in the prize ring, he who had raised the flagging spirits of the downtrodden Irish by his stirring victories over highly-regarded English boxers, he who had so impressed the Prince Regent with his courage and personality that he had allegedly been given the first knighthood ever awarded to a pugilist — could anyone be so evil as to deny their idol his well-earned sleep of peace?

The rumours which swept the country were substantiated in *Carrick's Morning Post* on February 23. A letter, written by J. Burrowes, of 73 Baggot Street, Dublin, disclosed: 'Having attended the remains of the victorious Donnelly to his last home on Sunday, a curiousity of again beholding his grave induced me, on passing that way this evening, to turn into the ground accompanied by two friends. On coming to the Hero's grave, what was our surprise to behold the clay thrown up, the coffin lid broken and the body gone. It immediately occurred to us that the Resurrectionists of York Street had paid him a visit. We passed through Kilmainham and were informed that during the last two nights a few admirers of his art had been there to protect him, but their naturally jovial disposition and the severity of the weather prompted them to make too frequent libations on the tomb of the departed champion and disabled them from perceiving or opposing those riflers of the House of Death'.

Denials that Donnelly's grave had been violated failed to pacify the angry public. Minor riots broke out and the authorities were afraid the trouble might escalate. The police were ordered to spare no efforts in bringing the perpetrators of the outrage to justice and in recovering the body.

Suspicion fell on many sides. Morgan O'Doherty, in a letter to *Blackwood's Magazine,* related how some Dublin students were beaten up by a group of men who blamed them for the foul deed. The writer added, in plain frustration: 'It is absolutely impossible to ascertain the facts about the whereabouts of Donnelly's body. You hear a thousand times a day that it has been taken to Edinburgh'.

A group of publican friends of the late champion attempted to cool passions by having a letter published in the *Freeman's Journal* of March 4 in which they claimed the story of the body-snatch was a hoax.

The letter read: 'An article appeared in *Carrick's Morning Post* with the signature of a respectable individual annexed, stating 'that the body had been removed from its place of interment. We, on Thursday the 24th, visited the grave and, having it opened, found the body safe and undisturbed. As a further security we have had a temporary arch erected over it'. It was signed by Patrick Cody, P. Bergin (Fleet Street), Joseph Bergin (Essex Street), R. Gregson (Moore Street), Peter Kelly (Wood Quay), Garrett Graham (Cook Street), Byrne (Cole's Lane Market) and Traynor (Bass Place). The last-named was a relative of Donnelly's and Gregson was a prominent English pugilist whose songs and poems became so famous that he was known as Bob Gregson P.P. (Poet to Pugilism). Gregson held the licence of a public house in Dublin at the time of Donnelly's death.

Which, then, of the letter writers told the truth? Neither the *Freeman's Journal* nor *Carrick's Morning Post* carried any further correspondence on the subject. True to exasperating form for newspapers at that time, neither thought it worthwhile to investigate the facts of the matter.

Had the newspapers of the early 1800s been as keen as their modern counterparts to obtain a scoop, they would have gone to great lengths to dig out the truth about Donnelly's body-snatching. Today, such a story would have merited huge banner headlines. Then, they had neither the resources nor the inclination to follow it up. Irish newspapers were numerous, but had very limited circulations, as the majority of the people were illiterate. Editors devoted most of their space to European and English news and had little of purely Irish interest, apart from lists of births, marriages and deaths and accounts of robberies, duels and executions, plus notices of arrivals and departures of the packet steamers. The poorer classes, even if they could read then, could hardly afford newspapers, some of which cost as much as five old pennies. Later in the nineteenth century, as more people learned to read, newspaper circulations began to increase and publishers were able to drop the price, in many cases, to as little as a penny.

Admittedly, the newspapers were preoccupied at the death around that time of a rather greater figure on the world stage than Dan Donnelly. On the evening of January 29, 1820, without suffering and with no return to the sanity which had deserted him ten years earlier, King George III died. For several weeks, the newspapers carried little else but reports of the event and its aftermath. England and Ireland now had a new king, George IV, although he had to wait until July 1821 to be crowned officially.

But back to Dan Donnelly — and the Sack-'em-Ups. Was the Irish champion's corpse snatched from its burial place for the high price it would fetch on a market made necessary by the anatomy schools' desperate shortage of 'working material'? Or was the whole story just the product of some evil-minded prankster?

Alas, the truth will never be known. For myself, I am prepared to accept that Donnelly's body was a prime target for the resurrectionists and that the story of its theft is factual. Might not the publican friends of the departed hero have written the letter denying the removal of the remains in order to save their own skins, for had they not been entrusted with arranging the guarding of the grave?

'Sack-'em-Ups', as the body-snatchers were commonly known, were extremely active in Ireland and Britain until the passing of the Second Anatomy Act of 1832, which gave freer licence to doctors, teachers of anatomy and bona fide medical students to dissect donated bodies.

Up to the introduction of the new Act, the only bodies allowed by law to be used at schools of anatomy were those of convicted murderers. Naturally, there was a far greater demand than supply. In Edinburgh, for instance, there was an annual average of eight hundred and fifty anatomy students — yet there were only about seventy criminal executions a year. The schools had, therefore, to go outside the law in order to properly train their pupils. Hence the need for the body-snatchers. Reprehensible though their ghoulish trade certainly was, the world of surgery and medicine felt it owed them some debt.

Most notorious of the Sack-'em-Ups operating in Britain were Burke and Hare who, in fact, were Irishmen. William Burke was born in Cork and William Hare was from Derry. This evil pair settled in Edinburgh, the centre for anatomical teaching, early in the 19th century and set up their grim partnership. Not content with digging open graves, they resorted to murder. They are known to have slain at least fifteen people within twelve months, and to have sold their bodies for surgical dissection. Burke was hanged in 1829 but Hare, who turned King's evidence, received a pardon and, blinded as a result of an accident, roamed the streets of London for many years.

In Dublin, it was Dan Donnelly's burial place, the Royal Hospital Fields — or Bully's Acre as it was more familiarly known — which was the happy hunting ground for the grave riflers. Frequent battles took place there between the Sack-'em-Ups and the Dead Watchers (relatives or friends of the deceased).

Many prominent professors and surgeons were in league with the resurrectionists. More than one paid dearly for his participation in the gruesome business. The son of Dr. Kirby, president of the Royal College of Surgeons in Dublin, was caught in the act of digging up a body and was shot dead by a close relative of the deceased.

A more prolonged and horrifying death was the fate of a well-known Dublin surgeon, Peter Harkin, who was disturbed one night while he and his henchmen opened a grave in the Bully's Acre. Harkin, in trying to make his escape from the irate friends and relatives of the dead man, had only managed to clamber up on the wall when his pursuers grabbed hold of one of his legs. His other leg, on the outside of the cemetery wall, was clung onto by his assistants and there, straddled on the high wall, Harkin was almost literally torn apart in a grisly tug-of-war.

Christopher Dixon, a porter at the Royal College of Surgeons, was an active resurrectionist. He was once spotted removing a body and a mob tied a rope around him and ducked him several times in the River Liffey. He was lucky to escape with his life. Not so fortunate was one of Dixon's successors, Luke Redmond, who was killed in a riot as he was about to ship a body to Scotland.

'Zozimus' (Michael Moran), the famed blind ballad singer who lived all his life in the Liberties area of Dublin, had a great fear that the body-snatchers would get him if he died alone in his rented room. In one of his ballads, he pleaded with his old friend 'Stony Pockets':

> Oh Stony, Stony,
> Don't let the Sack-'em-Ups get me,
> Send round the hat
> And buy me a grave.

Stony dutifully raised enough money to get Zozimus buried in the comparative safety of Glasnevin Cemetery.

If we are to accept the story of Dan Donnelly's removal from the grave, we learn that the body was eventually traced to the home of a Dublin surgeon named Hall.

A group of publican friends of the late champion — Donnelly himself had held the licences of four taverns in the city at different times — warned Dr. Hall that he faced grim consequences if he failed to return the remains to their rightful resting place. Hall at first refused but, after a violent argument, he yielded to the pressure. But he insisted that he be allowed to keep at least part of his prize 'catch'. He cut off the corpse's right arm.

While the hero's remains were once more laid to rest in the Bully's Acre, we are told, his severed arm was slipped away to Scotland, where it was coated with preservative and was used by students in medical classes at Edinburgh University for many years.

Towards the end of the last century, the boxer's limb was passed to a travelling circus owner, who made a tidy little sum from the odd exhibit on many tours of Britain.

In 1904, Hugh 'Texas' McAlevey, a well known Belfast

bookmaker and sports enthusiast, rediscovered the arm and brought it back to Ireland. It was on display at his public house, the Duncairn Arms, in Duncairn Gardens, Belfast, for many years before being relegated to the dusty attic of McAlevey's bookmaker's shop in Winetavern Street in the same city. Bernie Small, now a popular cabaret artiste in Belfast, can recall when, as a teenager working for McAlevey, he was warned against going up into the attic because 'Donnelly's ghost' haunted it.

On the bookmaker's death, the attic was cleared out and the arm was given to a Belfast wine merchant and sportsman, Tom Donnelly (no relation to the Irish champion). And, in 1953, it came nearer 'home' when James Byrne, Junior, proprietor of The Hideout public house in Kilcullen, County Kildare, put it on display alongside such relics as a landlord's crop (a reminder of the land war), a 1798 pike, and a flag carried in Daniel O'Connell's victory parade. Another exhibit is a cross made from matchsticks, gramophone needles and toothbrush handles by political internees at the nearby Curragh Military Camp during World War II.

The walls of The Hideout are adorned with newspaper cuttings and magazine articles telling the colourful story of the famed Irish prizefighter. Tall tales, too, some of them — like the caption on the sketch of Donnelly, looking like the first cousin to a gorilla, which claims that Dan's arms were the longest in the history of pugilism and that 'he could button his knee breeches without stooping'. There is nothing abnormal in the length of the arm displayed in the nearby glasscase. It is about the right size for a man of just under six feet, which Donnelly was. The arm span of the average man, from fingertip to fingertip, is the same as his height.

But is the arm displayed in the Kilcullen bar, two miles from the scene of Donnelly's greatest ring triumph, over Englishman George Cooper on the Curragh of Kildare, actually the severed limb of the great hero?

Who can tell for certain? I have given the accounts as I found them and I am in no position to pass final judgement. The present owner of 'Donnelly's arm', Jim Byrne, says he does not doubt its authenticity and one must, I feel, without any conclusive evidence to the contrary, respect his view.

I wonder if Dan's 'ghost' in that Belfast attic was minus his right arm? Was he making an earthly return in a forlorn quest to be re-united with the mighty arm which had earned him his fame? Perhaps.

James J. Byrne Junior, of The Hideout, in Kilcullen, County Kildare, holds his prized possession – the right arm of 'Sir' Dan Donnelly. The story goes that the limb was severed from the champion's corpse after it was dug up from the grave in the Bully's Acre at Kilmainham.

The view from Carlisle Bridge (later widened and renamed
O'Connell Bridge) in 1820, the year of Dan Donnelly's death.

TOWNSEND STREET, in the tough dockland area of Dublin, was the birthplace of Dan Donnelly in March, 1788. He was the ninth of seventeen children, including four sets of twins, born to his carpenter father Joseph and his mother in the thirty-six years they lived there. The doctor who attended the birth of Dan was allegedly so impressed by the baby's sturdy appearance that he told the proud mother: 'Mrs. Donnelly, this child will one day be the wonder of his country'. The story of the doctor's prophecy, if it can be accepted, was recalled by one of Dan's sisters at the time of his death in 1820.

The boxing champion's date of birth cannot be confirmed, as no documented record is available. Newspaper accounts varied his age at his death from 32 to 44, while the original inscription on his monument in Donnelly's Hollow at the Curragh, in County Kildare, stated that he was born in 1770. It is noticeable that this was altered to 1788 when a new tablet was installed there in later years. But most of the authoritative sources, including *Pugilistica, the history of British boxing,* by Henry Downes Miles, and Nat Fleischer's *Ring Record Book,* list Donnelly as being born in March, 1788.

Further support for this date is provided by Pierce Egan, perhaps the greatest of all boxing historians, who wrote in *Boxiana* in 1818: 'He (Donnelly) is gifted with prodigious strength, no lack of courage, a good knowledge of the science and backed with the prime advantages of youth, being under 30 years of age'.

Whatever about the doctor's allusion to the 'boy wonder', young Dan received no preferential treatment from his parents. Each child of the large family got an equal share of love and attention. They were tough times for the Donnellys. The eight shillings (40p) a week that the father earned as a carpenter could not always be guaranteed, as he suffered from bronchitis and was often out of work. There was no such thing then as sick pay.

As a boy, Dan was said to be 'serene and composed and he bore injury with patience'. Strongly-built and naturally

The original inscription (above) on the monument in
Donnelly's Hollow, on the Curragh of Kildare, stated that
the Irish champion was born in 1770. When a new stone
tablet was placed there in 1953 (below) the more generally
accepted year of his birth, 1788, was inscribed.

DAN DONNELLY, CHAMPION OF IRELAND,
BORN IN DUBLIN 1788, OCCUPATION CARPENTER
BEGAN RING CAREER BY BEATING TOM HALL,
BEFORE 20,000 FANS AT THE CURRAGH SEPT. 1814
HALL LEFT THE RING IN FOURTEENTH ROUND
CRYING FOUL, IN DEC. 1815 DONNELLY BEAT
GEORGE COOPER AT THE CURRAGH, THREE YEARS
LATER HE WENT TO ENGLAND AND
CHALLENGED ALL COMERS, IN A 34 ROUND
FIGHT HE BEAT TOM OLIVER WITH A
HEAVY BLOW ON THE EAR FOLLOWED BY
A CROSS BUTTOCK.

boisterous, he would nevertheless go to great lengths to avoid getting involved in fights. But this was a time of frequent pitched battles on the streets of Dublin, mainly between the rival gangs on opposite sides of the River Liffey, the Liberty Boys and the Ormond Boys. A knowledge of self-defence was a considerable asset.

At times Dan, forced into combat lest doubts be cast upon his courage, had to take on older, bigger boys and many a time his mother would be required to stem the flow from a bloody nose or provide words of comfort on his injured pride.

School held no great attraction for young Donnelly, no more than it did for most children, then or now. On countless occasions, his mother had to abandon her heavy household chores and take the reluctant boy by the hand to his classroom at George's Quay. Though of above average intelligence, his schooling has been described as 'irregular' and 'unfinished'.

The Donnellys were among the slightly luckier ones. They at least had a part-time breadwinner. Unemployment was rife throughout Ireland because of periodic trade depressions and poverty was exacerbated by high rents and low wages. 'Poverty, disease and wretchedness exist in every great town,' wrote Curwin, an Englishman who toured Ireland shortly after the Act of Union of Great Britain and Ireland in 1800, 'but in Dublin the misery is indescribable'.

Two years earlier, Rev. James Whitelaw, the rector of St. Catherine's Church in Thomas Street, carried out a population census of the city (he estimated it at 182,000) and was appalled at the living conditions of the poor. 'My assistants and I, undeterred by the dread of infectious diseases, undismayed by degrees of filth, stench and darkness inconceivable by those who have not experienced them, explored, in the burning summer months of 1798, every room of these wretched habitations from the cellar to the garret and on the spot ascertained their population'.

A single apartment of the poor rated from one to two shillings (5p to 10p) per week and, to ease the rent burden, two, three or four families would often share the room.

Whitelaw frequently found 'from ten to sixteen persons of both sexes and all ages in a room not fifteen feet square 'stretched on a wad of filthy straw, swarming with vermin and without any covering save the wretched rags that constituted their wearing apparel'.

Not surprisingly, crime was rife. Riots and robberies were frequent. Churches were robbed, shop windows smashed and the goods stolen. Children were snatched from their parents for the sake of their clothes and turned naked onto the streets. People were murdered for their rings and watches. Beggars were everywhere. The grim conditions left the population susceptible to fevers and there were frequent epidemics, the worst being from 1817 to 1819.

For those at the other end of the scale, the rich, Dublin was an attractive, popular city which boasted a brilliant social life. Little did young Dan Donnelly think that he would see both extremes at close hand.

For all his giddiness and lack of application to any given task, Dan had his compensatory qualities. He was never known to bear lasting grudges against anyone, even those who got the better of him in street scraps, and he was considerate to the needs of his poorer playmates. Mrs. Donnelly repeatedly acceded to his pleas for pieces of bread to give to his hungry pals. She made the small sacrifice gladly.

If Dan's early aversion to discipline and the good advice of others was to remain a characteristic for the rest of his short life, so too was his sense of compassion for his fellow man. At the height of his ring fame, he would not leave the fight scene until he had consoled his beaten opponent and checked his condition.

This most admirable quality was inherited from his grand-father, Daniel Donnelly, whose kindness was renowned far beyond the County Louth parish of Cooley, where he had a well-cultivated farm adequately stocked with cattle. Shelter for the orphan, the poor widow or the travelling stranger was never known to be refused at the Donnelly farm.

Old Daniel made sure his five sons had a good education and brought them up in the best traditions of charity, humility and true Christianity. When he died at a ripe old age, he was widely grieved.

The farm passed into the hands of the two eldest sons, Hugh and James. They were not as good at the job as their late father and it looked as if the family might have to find other means of survival. One of the boys, Joseph, later to become father of the famed prizefighter, accepted an offer to travel to Newry, in County Down, and learn the carpentry trade from a Scot, Arthur McDonnell, an old friend of the family.

While in Newry, Joseph met and married a member of the high-ranking Gore family. The couple moved a few miles south to Dundalk, where they set up home and Joseph went to work at his newly-learned trade. But, in response to a plea from his aged, widowed mother, he returned to the farm and stayed there until she died. Shortly afterwards, Joseph and his wife packed their few belongings and journeyed to Dublin, where they spent the rest of their days.

Townsend Street, where they settled, got its name simply from being the street at the end of the town. Up to the middle of the 17th century, the River Liffey had remained unwalled and the sea came right up to where the street is now situated. Between 1792 and 1819, it was also the site of Westmoreland Hospital, which specialised in the treatment of venereal disease. There is a certain irony about this, for the hospital closed in the same year that Townsend Street's most famous resident, Dan Donnelly, was fighting his toughest battle — to rid his body of the very disease in which it gave such valuable treatment.

As a youth, Dan found hurling, handball and other sporting pastimes more deserving of his energy and time than carpentry, into which trade he had followed his father on leaving school at the age of twelve. It did not take much persuasion by his out-of-work pals to make Dan give the job a miss for a day or two. Many a lecture he got from his despairing parents on his lack of application to work.

One of Dan's workmates at Connery's timber yard in Sir John Rogerson's Quay, where he served his apprenticeship, was Arthur Devlin, brother of Robert Emmet's housekeeper, Anne Devlin. Donnelly's strong patriotic spirit was fanned

No traffic congestion in city-centre Dublin in 1820, when this scene of Sackville Street (later renamed O'Connell Street) was captured. With Nelson's Pillar destroyed by bombers in 1966, only the magnificent General Post Office remains to remind us that this was once one of Europe's most elegant thoroughfares.

by his friendship with Arthur who, along with the rest of his family, were jailed for their part in the abortive uprising led by Emmet in 1803.

Dan, in his serious moments, would speak proudly of his love for his country and how he despised those who turned their backs on Ireland.

Most of the time, however, he was as cheerful a companion as anyone could hope for. There was rarely a dull moment with Dan. He was a great story-teller and was always ready to burst into song, dance a jig or go on a wild drinking spree. His cheerful disposition was, when he earned his fame in the prize-ring, to make him one of the most sought-after escorts in Ireland.

Although he was known to be handy with his fists whenever the need arose, he was, in reality, quite a mild-mannered youth. Almost impossible to provoke, he would go to great lengths to avoid settling an argument in the traditional Irish manner.

One thing that was guaranteed to upset Donnelly, was to see the old, the feeble or the underprivileged mistreated. Then, it was recorded, 'no lion could display more fury'.

Once he heard of an old woman who had died, poverty-stricken, in her lonely room not far from where he lived in Townsend Street. The woman's death was attributed to a highly-contagious fever. It was feared that anyone who went near the body would catch the fatal disease.

Donnelly was determined that the old woman would receive a decent burial and asked for help in removing the corpse. There were no volunteers. So he went alone to the dark, dingy tenement room, tied a rope around the crude coffin and hoisted it up on his back, then carried it to a local churchyard.

The church sexton was busy levelling the bottom of a newly-dug grave when he was startled by the shadow of the brawny youth carrying the coffin. When Donnelly told him he wished to bury the woman there, the sexton refused point blank. He said the grave was reserved for 'a person of distinction'.

Dan eyed the sexton sternly and, controlling his temper,

told him: 'If you don't stand aside, it is you who will be occupying this grave. This is a land of equality and this woman has as much right to be buried here as anyone'. The churchman offered no further resistance and stood aside as Donnelly lowered the coffin and filled in the grave.

On another occasion, Dan's role of Good Samaritan almost cost him his life, or at least might have prevented his ever earning fame as a boxer.

Late one night he was on his way home after leaving a Ringsend public house when he heard the terrified screams of a young woman. Though bemused after several hours' heavy drinking, he managed to trace the distress call to a dark alley. There he saw a teenage girl struggling desperately with two burly sailors.

The attackers dragged the girl to the dockside and tossed her into the murky waters. Donnelly did not hesitate. Slipping out of his jacket as he ran, he adroitly sidestepped the two seamen and plunged into the river. The girl was about 20 yards out by the time he swam to her side. She almost sank beneath his grasp but the gallant rescuer managed to get her ashore, only to find the ruffians waiting for him.

Dan, too exhausted from his swim to be able to put up much of a fight, was viciously punched, kicked and beaten with a stone until the two bullies had satisfied their wrath.

The young man was a mass of deep cuts and bruises when two passers-by picked him up. His arm was broken in four places when he had tried to ward off the stone used to batter him. The hospital physician despaired at the sight of the mangled arm.

'I am sorry,' he told Dan's distraught parents, who had been summoned to the hospital, 'but the arm will have to be amputated'.

Mr. and Mrs. Donnelly pleaded with him to try and save the limb. Doctor Abraham Colles, a man whose compassion and care for the city's poor was widely acknowledged and appreciated, was so impressed with what he was told of the youngster's own many acts of charity that he promised to do what he could.

With infinite patience and delicate skill, the doctor managed to piece together the shattered bone fragments until, his job successfully completed, he put his arm around the young hero's shoulders and proclaimed him 'a pocket Hercules'.

So another underprivileged Dublin family, the Donnellys, had cause to bestow their blessings on the beloved Dr. Colles. The Kilkenny-born medic came from a long line of surgeons and was twice president of the Royal College of Surgeons in Dublin.

After being conferred M.D. in Edinburgh, he spent some time in London and then returned to Dublin to teach anatomy and surgery at his rented rooms in South King Street. He was later appointed to the Dispensary for the Sick Poor in Meath Street and was district visitor to the Sick and Indigent Roomkeepers' Society.

A contemporary credited Dr. Colles with 'solid judgement, manly directness, perfect probity, the soundest of understandings and the kindest of hearts'. Widely acclaimed as a medical researcher and graphic lecturer, one of his papers on the fracture of a forearm bone was so highly considered that the term *Colles' fracture* is now used all over the world.

LIKE MANY of the famous names in ring history, Donnelly discovered, more by accident, than design, that he had the basic requirements of strength, courage and skill to equip himself as a boxer by being reluctantly drawn into a brawl with a bully. Appropriately, in Dan's case, his fighting 'debut' took place in a public house.

Then in his early twenties, he was enjoying a quiet drink after work with his ailing father, who took a sudden fit of violent coughing. A tough-looking sailor, who had just come ashore, derided the feeble, elderly man. Dan implored him to show some respect.

'Any cheek from you, me young bucko,' snapped the bully, 'and I'll teach you a lesson in respect'.

The youngster controlled his temper and asked only that they be left to finish their drink in peace. But the uncouth seaman continued to jeer the elder Donnelly until Dan, his patience finally exhausted, shouted at the tormentor: 'I have no desire to fight you, but if it is what you want I'll not back down'.

The ruffian placed his glass on the counter, wiped his mouth with his tattooed forearm and rushed at Donnelly. The youth stood his ground and met the charge with a tremendous right hand punch flush in the sailor's face. The bar counter shook under the impact of the big man as he was sent staggering back, the blood pouring from his nose.

Snarling, the seaman again attacked and, to his astonishment, found the young man fighting back with the fury of a lion. For fifteen minutes the two battled it out until, finally, the sailor slumped to the sawdust-strewn floor gasping 'Enough' through his bloody, swollen lips.

The news of how young Donnelly had tamed the bully spread swiftly through the neighbourhood. At every bar where he called for weeks afterwards, he was toasted as the hero of the area. One man who did not share the general acclaim was a local who had done some boxing and called himself the district champion. He threw out a challenge to Donnelly to prove who was the better man.

Dan would not hear of it. 'I have no wish to be classed as a fighting man,' he repeatedly told those who asked would he accept the challenge. It was only when word spread that he was afraid of the other man that he yielded to the pressure. The match was arranged and Dan beat his rival so severely that the loser expressed the parting hope that they would never meet again.

All of Dublin now heard about the boxing ability of this strong youngster from Townsend Street. Numerous challenges were presented to him. All he politely declined.

One boxer who was recognised as Champion of the City was jealous of the newcomer's reputation and was determined to test him out. He followed Donnelly to all his favourite drinking haunts and repeatedly demanded a fight. For some time Dan declined until, one night, his pursuer called him a coward before his friends. He agreed to the match, which was arranged for six days later on the banks of the Grand Canal in Dublin.

The contest aroused considerable interest throughout the city and a fair-sized crowd turned up to witness the bout and small wagers were made on the outcome. Right up to the time the boxers took up sparring positions, Donnelly continued to try to talk his rival out of fighting. His pleas were in vain.

In the early rounds, Donnelly's reluctance to do battle was obvious. He fought mainly on the retreat, trying to block or avoid his opponent's heavy blows. Only when he saw that the contest was likely to be prolonged did he become more aggressive. Dan gradually gained the upper hand and, in a furious attack in the 16th round, he beat his man to the turf to end the fight. He was now undisputed Champion of the City.

There were no further challenges, which pleased him no end.

Around this time, a conversation took place at a tavern in England between two pugilists and two members of the Fancy, as followers of boxing were then known. The prize-fighters poured scorn on Ireland's reputation as a nation of courageous men. They said they had gone there and issued

open challenges to the best boxers the country could produce
but had not found any acceptors.

One of the fans was Captain William Kelly, who ran a
race-horse training establishment at Maddenstown, in County
Kildare. A keen follower of boxing, he was stung at the
affront to his native land and resolved to find a fighting Irishman who would disprove the English boxers' charge. His
companion, a Scotsman named Robert Barclay Allardice,
better known as 'Captain Barclay' agreed to help Kelly in
his quest.

The pair travelled to Dublin, where they heard of the
promise shown by Dan Donnelly. But, they were warned,
they would have quite a job persuading him to enter the
prize-ring.

Sure enough, on meeting Kelly and Barclay, the amiable
carpenter showed no great enthusiasm for their plans.

'I am sorry if I have wasted your time, gentlemen,' said
Dan, 'but I am a man of peace'.

Kelly, the jibes of the English pugilists still ringing in his
ears, was not ready to concede defeat. He used every possible
ploy in his efforts to get Dan to change his mind. He recalled
stirring tales of how ancient Irish heroes had shed their blood
in defence of their country's honour. He told Donnelly how
much his country would be indebted to him if he wiped out
the slur cast by the two English boxers. Besides, concluded
Kelly, there was good money to be earned from the ring.

Dan was silent for a few moments. He told the two men
he would think over their offer and give his decision in a few
days. When they returned, he gave what seemed to be a well-
rehearsed speech.

'Gentlemen,' he said, 'I shall first return to you my sincere
thanks for the great dependence you have on my fidelity
towards my country. The honour you have conferred on me
shall ever be cherished in my bosom. To appear before a
multitude of spectators on a plain is wholly against my
will — yet my country claims my support'.

Holding up his right fist, he concluded: 'I owe no spleen to
Britain, but the man of any nation who presumes to offer an
insult to my country, this arm, while my life blood flows

shall defy'.

The delighted Kelly and Barclay applauded Donnelly's statement and promised him he would receive the full benefit of their experience and teaching.

Several other versions of how Donnelly was 'discovered' by Captain Kelly have been handed down, the most popular being that which claims that Kelly, quite by accident, saw Dan demolish a bar-full of men with a single blow each and was so impressed that he took the all-conquering hero in hand there and then.

The most fanciful of all accounts, however, is undoubtedly that by Malachi Horan, the wonderful old story-teller from Killenarden, in County Wicklow. The yarn is recorded in a book by Dr. George A. Little, one-time president of the Old Dublin Society, entitled *Malachi Horan Remembers.* The story, for all its improbabilities, is worth repeating. This was how the old story-teller related it, in his own quaint colourful way:

'Dan Donnelly was a hedge carpenter, out of Dublin. He was a big, loose man, like a reaping hook. He travelled this road and every road looking for work. One day and him passing Captain Kelly's of Valleymount*, he looked over the fence and saw the captain and him taking a beating from a rough-looking martyr. Captain Kelly was a great man for the boxing; he had half the country fighting. After him watching a bit, Donnelly could stand it no longer. He up and shouts to the Captain: 'Eh, man, will you go in and fight and stop waiting to be beat'. That seemed to freshen up the Captain for he downed his man. All over, he came up to Donnelly and asked him would he have a fancy to try his hand. Donnelly, who saw his dinner in it, took the chance quick enough.

'Boys-o-boys, that was the sore day in Valleymount. It was like ninepins the way Dan knocked down every man put up to him by Captain Kelly. It was not only his dinner that Donnelly got on the head of it; no indeed, for the Captain hired him to work about the place. Of course, the

---

* *Malachi Horan is misquoted here. He obviously was referring to Ballymount, County Kildare, not Valleymount, County Wicklow.*

Right — Robert Barclay Allardice, known as 'Captain Barclay', in his walking costume. He once walked 210 miles in three days. Acknowledged as the first tutor to recognise the benefits of correct training for a fight, among those who benefited from his strict regimen were Dan Donnelly, Tom Cribb, John Gully and Tom Oliver.

Captain Barclay.

Pub. May 3. 1813 by. R. S. Kirby, 11 London house Yard.

fighting was Captain Kelly's object, for he was the great trainer.

'The Captain near burst with interest teaching Donnelly; but not a mite more than his sister, Miss Kelly. Clean crazy she was about Donnelly's fighting. And Dan repaid them well. As sure as there is tinkers in Wicklow, he had every man in the country beat before they knew he was in it. And not a hair out of Donnelly either. Soon there was nothing left for him to beat...'

Malachi Horan, who was born in 1847, at the time of the Great Famine, deplored the fact that Donnelly was not around at the same time as Simon Byrne, a renowned Irish heavyweight who campaigned between 1825 and 1833.

'Gor-a-wor, but that would have been a match,' enthused the old story-teller. 'A quiet, easy-going lad was Simon, but tough as a furze and clean as a whip. Ah, it is the pity of the world that he never fought Dan Donnelly'. Simon Byrne, incidentally, was so badly beaten in his last fight by James (Deaf) Burke, a brutal battle lasting three hours and sixteen minutes, that he died from his injuries.

Captain Kelly installed Donnelly at his brother's residence in Calverstown, near the Curragh of Kildare. There he learned the rudiments of fighting skill and the proper methods of training from Kelly's friend, Captain Barclay. He could not have been in better hands.

Barclay, a patron of two of the greatest English bare-knuckle champions, John Gully and Tom Cribb, was acknowledged as one of the foremost boxing trainers of his day. He was quite a remarkable man in many other ways, too.

Member of Parliament for the County of Kincardine for three successive parliaments, he was an intimate friend of William Pitt 'the Younger', the Prime Minister who effected the Union of Great Britain and Ireland in 1800. Barclay also claimed the title Earl of Monteith and Airth.

Over six feet tall, handsome and well-built, Barclay was famed as an athlete and often sparred with the boxers he trained. An immensely strong man, it was said at the age of twenty he lifted a man of eighteen stone from floor to table with one hand. He won many wagers for his outstanding walking feats. On one occasion he covered the distance from London to Ury (five hundred and ten miles) in ten days and he is also recorded as having walked eighty-one miles in under sixteen hours. Barclay died in 1854 at the age of seventy-five from the effects of a kick in the head by a horse.

Donnelly, while training under Captain Barclay at Calverstown Demesne, earned his keep by working as a cowman. Up to quite recent years, the building which was Dan's training quarters was used as a hen run. It had very high walls and no roof and was in a bad state of disrepair when the present owner of Calverstown House, Mr. P. J. McCall, had it demolished and replaced it with stables.

Donnelly's initials were supposed to have been carved on rafters at Calverstown but there is no trace of them today. Probably they were in the old buildings that were pulled down after Mr. McCall bought Calverstown House from the late Otway Freeman in 1958. The present owner recalls two huge dumb-bells lying about the place when he took it over. They were most likely part of Dan's training equipment, for he did use dumb-bells to build up his strength. But, when last seen, they were in a bad state of woodworm and were probably disposed of for that reason.

Whatever about the value of Donnelly's learning his boxing skills from Captain Barclay, it is not so certain that he did well to come under the patronage of the eccentric Captain William Kelly.

One of the mad Kellys of Maddenstown, whose favourite diversion was reputed to be dancing in their pelts, William was certainly an extraordinary character. Known as 'Sporting' Captain Kelly, he would wager on such idiotic happenings as which of two flies would leave a wall first.

Maddenstown House, Captain Kelly's residence in County Kildare, was known up to recent years as Cooper's ruins — undoubtedly so named as a grim reminder of the battered state of George Cooper after the Englishman was beaten by Donnelly in their epic battle on the Curragh.

The ruins were demolished to build a new house for the present owner of the site, famed racehorse trainer, P. J.

"SPORTING" CAPT. WM. KELLY
of the Curragh of Kildare.
COPIED FROM PAINTING IN POSSESSION OF HIS GRANDDAUGHTER, MRS BAILIE

*'Sporting' Captain William Kelly, the man credited with 'discovering'
Donnelly and launching him on his short-lived ring career. A racehorse
owner and trainer, Kelly was a talented performer on the uileann pipes,
which he played before King George IV when the monarch visited
Ireland in 1821.*

Prendergast. He recalls that, before pulling down the old building, there was a lot of filling-in work to do where there appeared to be underground kitchens and cellars.

Captain Kelly's successes with horses are renowned. He also earned some fame as a musician. A talented performer on the bagpipes, he played before King George IV on the occasion of the monarch's visit to Ireland in 1821, using a set of uileann pipes previously presented to him by the same personage while he was Prince Regent.

The magnificent ebony set of pipes, tipped with ivory and with silver-plated mountings, was engraved 'William Kelly Esq., 1809' and was on display at Kilkea Castle, Castledermot, County Kildare, until recent years. Its present whereabouts are unknown.

Kilkea Castle, an 1849 reconstruction of a medieval castle associated with Gerald, the famous Wizard (eleventh) Earl of Kildare, was in more recent years the seat of the FitzGeralds, Dukes of Leinster. It is now an hotel.

A measure of Kelly's ability to pass on his musical talents is borne out by the fame achieved by some of his pupils, among them the renowned 'Kildare Piper', Johnny Hicks, whose performance delighted audiences in Britain and the United States as well as in his native country. Captain Francis O'Neill, in his book *Irish Minstrels and Musicians,* said of Kelly: 'If we are to judge the teacher by the style and execution of those who graduated under his tuition, the renowned turfman must be ranked among the best pipers of the day'.

Like himself, two of William's brothers achieved ranking positions in the British Army. Colonel Ponsonby Kelly commanded the 24th Regiment and Captain Waldron Kelly served in the 41st Regiment. His first cousin, Col. Edward Kelly, 'performed brilliant service on the field at Waterloo'.

Because of his affection for the pipes, William named several of his horses after parts of them, such as Drone, Chanter and Bellows. A particularly fine grey horse was Drone and his successes are recorded in the racing calendars of the period.

Kelly, born at New Abbey House in Co. Kildare around

the year 1780, married his first cousin, a Miss Orford, of Rathbride Manor, and had seven sons and one daughter. After a long and brilliant career on the turf, he retired to his town house, in The Crescent, Clontarf, and died there around 1858. A child neighbour of his was Bram Stoker, who became a civil servant and later wrote the classic horror novel *Dracula*. Stoker, who for nearly thirty years was secretary to Sir Henry Irving, the acknowledged 'king' of Victorian melo-drama, was born at No. 15, The Crescent, in 1847.

If Captain Kelly's renowned patriotic pride helped boost Dan Donnelly's intense spirit of nationalism, it is equally certain that his fondness for the 'wild life' also rubbed off on the impressionable boxer.

Nevertheless, Donnelly applied himself well to the task of learning the Manly Art and soon his backers were convinced he was ready to take the test.

A challenge was issued to Tom Hall, a prominent English pugilist who was touring Ireland giving sparring exhibitions and instruction in the sport. Hall had never heard of Donnelly and therefore saw the contest as an easy way to supplement his earnings. He accepted the invitation without hesitation.

The match was arranged for the Curragh of Kildare on September 14, 1814. The purse money was to be a hundred guineas, sixty for the winner and forty for the loser.

Many of the Donnelly's friends thought he was too severely tried on his first outing under the patronage of Captain Kelly. Hall, born at Newport on the Isle of Wight in 1791, was three years younger than the Dublin carpenter but he had considerably more ring experience. He had been described as 'the most courageous pugilist in England' and numbered among his victims George Cribb, brother of the legendary Tom Cribb, champion of England.

Donnelly's advice to those who doubted his chances was: 'Don't bet too much on me, then you won't lose too much if I am beaten'. But he did not seriously consider the possibility of defeat. To those who confided that they were prepared to wager heavily on his success, he boasted he would 'rather die than yield to Tom Hall'.

In fact, so cocksure was he that he felt he need not stick too rigidly to the training rules laid down by his backers. Part of his routine was regular early morning walks through the fields around Calverstown and then back to his training quarters for breakfast.

Many a time in the three weeks of so-called intensive training for the fight, Dan would not show up for his morning meal. Search parties would eventually track him down to a village tavern where he would join in drinking sessions with his growing band of admirers. Bad enough for a man with an empty stomach, but disastrous for an athlete in training.

Captain Kelly set up a wide network of 'spies' to make sure Donnelly was kept away from the villages and the well-meant attentions of his supporters. All things considered, Dan was in remarkably good condition on the day of the fight.

LL ROADS TO the Curragh on the morning of September 14, 1814, were jammed with coaches, jaunting cars, gigs, carts and drays, men on horseback and those who had no means of transport. Many gladly walked the thirty miles from Dublin to see the battle between Donnelly and Hall. Black-shawled widows, clutching the hands of their under-nourished bare-footed offspring, chattered excitedly with fellow pedestrians along the way. It helped relieve the monotony of the long journey.

By one o'clock in the afternoon, when the bout was due to start, an estimated twenty thousand people filled every available inch of the hollow, at the base of which a twenty-two foot square had been roped off. The hillsides formed a natural amphitheatre, so that everyone had a good view of the ring. It was not the first prizefight to be held there. The spot was then known as Belcher's Hollow, after Englishman Tom Belcher's victory there over an Irish lightweight named Dan Dougherty in April, 1813.

To this day, however, the place is known as Donnelly's Hollow.

The extraordinary interest generated by the fight between Donnelly and Hall can be partially explained by the public's fondness for brutal, blood-letting spectacles. The chief amusements of the period included such grotesque 'sports' as cock-fighting, bull-baiting and dog fights, all of which were the subject of heavy betting, as with prize-fighting. Public executions always drew huge audiences.

Pugilism contained enough savagery and blood to satisfy the most sadistic onlooker. Unlike modern boxing, where heavily-padded gloves reduce the incidence of severe facial cuts as well as providing protection for the hands, which are also carefully bandaged, bare-knuckle fighting often wreaked considerable and permanent damage on both victor and vanquished.

Broken fingers, torn muscles and sprained wrists were as common among winning boxers as were fractured noses, broken ribs and concussion among the defeated men.

Blows to the eyes, the side of the neck and to the throat

Right — Jack Broughton's Rules drawn up in 1743 lasted 110 years until replaced by the London Prize Ring Rules. The seven simple guidelines left a great deal to the individual judgement of referees. The illustrations show that, while prize-fights were fought with bare knuckles, gloves or 'mufflers' were employed for practice or exhibition matches.

THE RING

RULES

TO BE OBSERVED IN ALL BATTLES ON THE STAGE

I. THAT a square of a Yard be chalked in the middle of the Stage; and on every fresh set-to after a fall, or being parted from the rails, each Second is to bring his Man to the side of the square, and place him oppofite to the other, and till they are fairly set-to at the Lines, it fhall not be lawful for one to ftrike at the other.

II. That, in order to prevent any Difputes, the time a Man lies after a fall, if the Second does not bring his Man to the fide of the square, within the fpace of half a minute, he fhall be deemed a beaten Man.

III. That in every main Battle, no perfon whatever fhall be upon the Stage, except the Principals and their Seconds; the fame rule to be obferved in bye-battles, except that in the latter, Mr. Broughton is allowed to be upon the Stage to keep decorum, and to affift Gentlemen in getting to their places, provided always he does not interfere in the Battle; and whoever pretends to infringe thefe Rules to be turned immediately out of the houfe. Every body is to quit the Stage as foon as the Champions are ftripped, before the fet-to.

IV. That no Champion be deemed beaten, unlefs he fails coming up to the line in the limited time, or that his own Second declares him beaten. No Second is to be allowed to afk his man's Adverfary any queftions, or advife him to give out.

V. That in bye-battles, the winning man to have two-thirds of the Money given, which fhall be publicly divided upon the Stage, notwithftanding any private agreements to the contrary.

VI. That to prevent Difputes, in every main Battle the Principals fhall, on coming on the Stage, choofe from among the gentlemen prefent two Umpires, who fhall abfolutely decide all Difputes that may arife about the Battle; and if the two Umpires cannot agree, the faid Umpires to choofe a third, who is to determine it.

VII. That no perfon is to hit his Adverfary when he is down, or feize him by the ham, the breeches, or any part below the waift: a man on his knees to be reckoned down.

As agreed by feveral Gentlemen at Broughton's Amphitheatre,
Tottenham Court Road, Auguft 16, 1743.

were considered particularly damaging, whereas today the knockout artist aims for the point of the chin or the angle of the jaw if he wants an early night. In *Mendoza's Modern Art of Boxing*, published around 1792, the author listed as one of the most telling punches that delivered 'under the short ribs or in the kidneys, as it is termed, which deprives the person struck of his breath, occasions an instant discharge of urine, puts him in the greatest torture and renders him for some time a cripple'.

All bare-fist battles were to a finish, only ending when one man was beaten unconscious or conceded defeat, or if nightfall or the attentions of the law intervened. Rounds were not of equal length as they are today, but lasted until one or both of the boxers was knocked down or fell to the ground. If one contestant failed to toe the 'scratch line' in the centre of the ring after the thirty-second rest following a knockdown, then he was declared the loser.

So if one reads of a bare-knuckle fight lasting for sixty rounds or more, the actual amount of time spent could be less than a modern fifteen-round contest (each round now lasting a specified three minutes). Some of the old prizefights lasted only a bare minute or two, while others dragged on for several hours. It was common practice for a tired boxer to go down on one knee after a light blow and thus gain a much-needed half-minute rest.

Nevertheless, the battles could be vicious and there was nothing to prevent a fighter bashing his opponent's head against a wooden corner post, elbowing him in the face or getting a stranglehold around his neck with one arm and punching him to the face with his free hand. The rules of boxing as drawn up by Jack Broughton in 1743 did not forbid butting, eye-gouging, hair-pulling or wrestling.

Broughton's Rules governed boxing until 1838, when they were replaced by the London Prize Ring Rules. These were revised in 1853 and supplanted in 1867 by the Marquis of Queensberry Rules which, with some modifications, stand to this day.

It should be noted that if Broughton's Rules had been strictly interpreted in Dan Donnelly's fight with Tom Hall,

Jack Broughton, Champion of England, who in 1743 formulated the first set of boxing rules, see page 41, and invented the boxing glove, which at the time was only used in sparring exhibitions. Broughton lived to the ripe old age of 85 and was one of the last non-Royals to be buried at Westminster Abbey.

the Irishman should have lost the contest.

First to enter the ring, to thunderous applause, Donnelly looked the picture of calmness and confidence. So intent was he on the job ahead that he appeared not to notice the excited wellwishers who slapped him on the back and shouted 'Good luck, Dan'.

Hall followed some minutes later and threw his hat into the ring, signifying his readiness to do battle. He ducked under the rope, walked up to Donnelly and shook his hand. Then he bowed respectfully to the audience and addressed them with a well-prepared speech. 'Gentlemen of Ireland,' he began, 'I come here not to shed contempt on your country; if I did, I would not consider myself worthy of calling myself a man'.

'England is the place of my birth,' he told the hushed crowd, 'and nature has designed me to gain a living by the power of my arm. My profession, therefore, is that of a pugilist, to whom all countries are alike. The man of any nation who professes the same character is the man for me. Therefore, I hope your hospitable hearts will not be moved to envy me, as the stranger who now has the honour of standing before you means not to degrade the land of Erin, but to try his strength with a man'.

His eloquent words were greeted with loud cheers. The contestants 'took a glass together' and then stripped. It was noticeable that the Irishman was much the taller and heavier of the two. In fact, Donnelly, at half an inch under six feet and weighing 14 stone, was a good three inches taller and over two stone heavier than Hall, who was little more than a middleweight in modern boxing terms.

Donnelly was seconded by his backers, Captain Kelly and Captain Barclay, while Hall had two wellknown English prizefighters, Jack Carter and Ned Painter, in his corner. The betting odds were six to four on the Englishman. It was generally assumed that his greater experience and skill would be too much for the raw Dubliner.

A newspaper account noted that 'several very respectable females were seated among the crowd,' evidence of the sex appeal of the handsome hero who carried the hopes of the

Irish on his wide shoulders.

This serves to expose the following, that it was the good-looking Frenchman Georges Carpentier who first attracted women to watch boxing matches, just before the start of World War I. Later, handsome heavyweights like Max Baer, Len Harvey and Ireland's own 'broth of a boy' Jack Doyle all commanded sizeable female followings. But here is evidence that brave battlers with bulging muscles set feminine hearts a-flutter long before the arrival of 'Georgeous Georges'. Donnelly's rugged good looks, his brawny build and his ready wit made him a popular figure with the opposite sex. And he wasn't slow to cash in on the benefits.

Donnelly and Hall walked to the centre of the ring and again shook hands, as did their respective seconds. It was 1 p.m. as the contest began and 'a solemn silence prevailed'.

The contrast in styles was marked by the Irishman's straight-up, unvarying stance and Hall's lower posture and greater flexibility.

Both men opened cautiously, their eyes fixed steadfastly on each other. Donnelly attempted the first punch, a left that was blocked by Hall. The Englishman attempted a counter blow but missed. The pair went into a clinch. Several hits were exchanged before Hall fell to the ground to end the first round, which had lasted one minute.

The second round saw Hall on the retreat, trying to draw the inexperienced Irishman into leaving his guard open. His tactics paid off. As Hall ducked a ponderous swing, he countered with a severe blow to split Donnelly's lip. The Englishman had drawn 'first blood', considered an important stage in a bare-fist fight and usually a point of heavy betting in itself.

Donnelly, his pride hurt as much as his person, quickly regained the upper hand and again brought Hall to his knees to end the round. The pattern for the next three rounds was Hall retreating, Donnelly chasing and each time it was the visitor who dropped to the turf.

Hall opened the sixth round in more determined fashion. He stood and traded punches with the bigger man until, beaten back against the ropes, he would have fallen but for the strands supporting him. He still tried to match Donnelly blow for blow but finally fell exhausted. It was the liveliest round so far.

Both men went down in a tangle to end the seventh and Dan showed signs of losing his temper when Hall dropped without being hit to climax the next round. He drew back his foot as if to kick his kneeling rival but was restrained by Captain Kelly, who yelled: 'Are you mad, Dan? Do you want to lose the fight?'

It was plainly evident by now that Hall was no match for the bigger, stronger man. He was floored by heavy smashes in the ninth and tenth rounds and, in the next, a heavy left to the eye left him kneeling dejectedly on the turf.

The visitor somehow rallied briefly to match Donnelly's efforts in the twelfth round, but the fierce exchange took too much out of him and he again dropped to his knees.

Hall, now visibly distressed and breathing in deep gasps, was knocked down twice more before, in the fifteenth round, he backed to the ropes and a tremendous right from Donnelly grazed his chin. The punch did not land properly but Hall sunk to the ground, as much from exhaustion as from fear of his attacker's follow-up attempts.

Donnelly, his patience finally ebbed, lashed out with a vicious right that caught the kneeling visitor on the side of the head and brought blood from his ear. It was an obvious foul and Hall's seconds jumped into the ring demanding that he be named the winner. Donnelly's handlers maintained that Hall was well beaten and deserved to lose for going down so often without being struck. They insisted their man's final punch was accidentally landed while Hall was down.

Hall's cornermen refused to let their boxer continue. And so ended, in bitter dispute, Donnelly's eagerly awaited big test against English opposition.

The general opinion around the ringside was that the purse money should be evenly divided between the two contestants or that they should fight again. It was then decided to leave the verdict to 'the noblemen and gentlemen of the Irish Turf Club'.

A letter in *Carrick's Morning Post* on September 22, eight

days after the fight, stated that the Turf Club had decided that 'bets depending on the match between Donnelly and Hall be withdrawn and the purse should be divided between the contestants, both having deviated from the technical line of fair play'. It was also announced that Donnelly was to fight Jack Carter, who had seconded Hall, at the Curragh in the following April.

Two days later, in the same paper, a letter signed by 'An Amateur' claimed that nothing had been decided and, as the Turf Club could not come to an understanding, it had been agreed to refer the matter to the members of the Pugilistic Club in London. The letter added that rumours of a match between Donnelly and Carter were unfounded.

Regrettably, the newspaper dropped the controversy at this juncture and no further mention is made of whether the Pugilistic Club reached a decision. It is likely they felt the issue was outside their jurisdiction, having taken place in Ireland.

Whatever the claims and counter-assertions, there was no doubt in the minds of Donnelly's supporters as to who had won the battle of the Curragh. Every village within miles of the fight venue re-echoed the cheers as news reached them of the Irishman's 'victory'. Farmers' boys who had saved for six months to buy new suits recklessly spent the money on drinking toasts to their idol. In many parts of Ireland, bonfires were lit and people sang and danced around them in celebration.

As for Dan himself, he was on his way back to Calverstown after the fight when his coach was stopped by adoring fans. The horses were unyoked and the crowd jostled for the honour of drawing the vehicle themselves. The Irish Champion, as he was now acclaimed, revelled in his new-found fame and gladly joined in the drinking sprees that made small fortunes for publicans throughout County Kildare for the following week.

It was fully eight days before Dan managed to tear himself away from his still rejoicing companions. He had expressed a wish to return to Dublin to see his mother, now a widow, and his brothers and sisters.

No sooner did he arrive home in Townsend Street when a huge throng carried him off to further celebrations at a local tavern. Dan sang, danced and told and re-told his version of the fight until the party ended the following morning.

After a few days' much-needed rest, Donnelly was back at work in the carpenter's shop. Not one penny had he to show as his proceeds from the fight against Hall a fortnight earlier.

Tom Molyneux, the American born slave who was one of the first black boxers to achieve world fame. He twice lost in savage battles with English champion Tom Cribb. Molyneux challenged Dan Donnelly to a fight in 1815, but the Irish champion refused the match, much to the American's disgust. Like Donnelly, Molyneux was too fond of drink and, as with Dan, he died in his early thirties. Molyneux was buried in Galway.

ON JUNE 18, 1815, near the village of Waterloo, eight miles south of Brussels, Napoleon's French forces were defeated in battle by a combined force of British, German, Dutch, and Belgian soldiers, led by the Duke of Wellington. News of the great battle was still echoing around the world a month later when a friend of Donnelly's dropped into his workplace one afternoon to tell him two gentlemen were waiting to meet him in a local tavern. Dan put down his wooden mallet and immediately went to the bar. He ordered a pint of porter (a dark malt liquor similar to stout, but cheaper and not as strong) and stood by the counter.

One of the strangers, a black man, approached him. 'Sir, I perceive you are Mr. Donnelly,' he ventured. When Dan confirmed his identity, the visitor introduced himself and his companion. 'This is George Cooper and I am Tom Molyneux. We are in Ireland on an exhibition tour and to teach the art of boxing. We have been told you are the best man in Ireland and I would like to challenge you to a match'.

Dan did not answer right away. He felt honoured that two such illustrious prizefighters had paid him a visit, but decided that there would be little glory in defeating Molyneux, who had only recently been beaten by the other man present, Cooper.

'No, I do not wish to fight a conquered man,' he said firmly, 'but I am willing to meet Mr. Cooper if he so desires'.

Molyneux, stung at the curt dismissal of his challenge, began to insult the Irish champion. He was calmed, however, by Cooper, who smilingly shook Donnelly's hand and said he would be happy to do battle with him.

A sad postscript to the meeting of the three boxers was the way in which Molyneux, already a heavy drinker, sank steadily into decay. He was taken ill while touring the West of Ireland with a boxing show in 1818 and died in the barrack rooms of the 77th infantry Regiment, stationed in Galway. He was thirty-four years of age.

It was a particularly sad end for the man who, born a slave on a Virginia plantation, had the effrontery to twice claim the championship of England, and only to lose to the legitimate titleholder, Tom Cribb, in two savage battles.

Donnelly's supporters were delighted to hear the news of his planned meeting with George Cooper. The Irish champion, however, privately admitted to some misgivings. Cooper had a formidable reputation and his renowned scientific ability would be hard to combat.

A native of Stone in Staffordshire, Cooper was known as 'The Bargeman' because he worked as a labourer on canal boats. Of gypsy blood, he is said to be the man on whom George Borrow based his character, 'the Flaming Tinman', in *Romany Rye*. Rated one of the most complete boxers of his time, Cooper could hit hard and fast with both hands, was noted for his skilful use of the 'one, two', was adept at blocking and countering and topped all this with an ample supply of courage. Bill Richmond, the great black boxer, called him 'the best natural fighter I have worked with'.

If there was one flaw in Cooper's make-up, it was his aversion to training. This could hardly be considered advantageous to Donnelly, whose own preparation for a fight, according to one prominent British writer some years later, 'appears to have consisted of limiting himself to 25 glasses of whiskey a day'. Exaggerated and derisive though the comment may have been, it was certainly true that the tavern held more attraction than the training camp for the devil-may-care Dubliner.

Boredom with the routine of training and the long, lonely walks that Captain Barclay prescribed were the perils that Donnelly found difficult to evade. Wisely, Captain Kelly made sure his wealthy friends in County Kildare regularly entertained the boxer during his leisure hours. Too close contact with the adoring peasantry would have been fatal to his chances of success against Cooper.

From early morning on the day of the fight, December 13, 1815, the roads to the Curragh were thronged despite the rain which fell steadily until daybreak. No one had to ask the way, as all were headed for the same place, Donnelly's Hollow.

As for the fight with Tom Hall fifteen months before, it

George Cooper, Donnelly's opponent in the famous battle on the Curragh of Kildare in December, 1815. Known as 'The Bargeman' because of his job on canal boats, Cooper, from Stone, in Staffordshire, was rated a first-rate ringman, being a hard and fast puncher, adept at blocking and countering and backing this with great courage.

seemed as if every horse-drawn vehicle to be found was used to transport eager fans to the battle scene. Those who had no means of conveyance or were unable to hitch a lift gladly completed the journey on foot. Again, some twenty-thousand spectators packed the site by ten o'clock, when the bout was due to commence.

A last-minute dispute over the purse money caused some delay and almost led to the match being called off. The original agreement was that the winner would receive £100 and the loser £20. Cooper was understandably angry when, on his arrival, he was told that the funds raised were not enough to cover the initial terms. It would now be £60 for the victor and nothing for the man who lost.

The Englishman refused to go through with the contest under these conditions and he sat in his chaise for almost an hour while the wrangle continued. Word of the row spread through the crowd and there were fears of a riot if the contest was cancelled. Cooper was advised, in the interests of his health and safety, he had better fight.

The multitude, though supporters of the Irish champion almost to a man, did not allow their hero-worship cloud their judgement as to the way the fight might go. Plenty of Irish money was wagered on the visitor, who was named two-to-one favourite.

Polite applause greeted Cooper's appearance in the ring, while the thunderous cheers that met Donnelly's arrival could be heard in villages several miles away. The crowd's excitement was at fever pitch as they awaited the start.

Ned Painter, who had seconded Hall in his bout with Donnelly, again appeared in the rival corner. The Irishman was attended by Jack Coady. When the contestants 'came to scratch', it was noticeable that Dan once again had the advantage in height and weight over his opponent. Cooper, 5 ft. 10 ins. tall and weighing 12 stone, was almost two inches the shorter man and two stone the lighter.

Both men looked surprisingly fit, considering their renowned hatred of training. Donnelly's condition, particularly, was a tribute to the patience and perseverance of his trainer, Captain Barclay. It is true to say that had Dan

taken such care of his physical wellbeing from then on, he
would have enjoyed a longer boxing career — and extended
his life period. Alas, such concern was not part of his
makeup.

The fight began with preliminary sparring before Donnelly
landed the first punch, a heavy hook to the Englishman's
neck. Cooper replied with a solid dig to the body. They went
to close quarters and 'desperate milling' ended with
Donnelly, his superior strength already showing, knocking
his rival to the ground.

In his colourful account of the knockdown in *Boxiana,*
Pierce Egan wrote: 'It would be impossible to describe the
shout that accompanied this feat; it was not unlike the fire
of artillery and the faces of the Paddies smiled again with
innate approbation'.

In round two, both men displayed considerable defensive
skill and it was some time before the first blow was struck, 'a
sharp facer' from Donnelly. A follow-up punch made
Cooper's ear bleed. 'First blood' to the local man — and first
bets settled. Donnelly drove Cooper to the ropes and again
floored him.

Cries of 'Bravo, Dan' and 'Ireland for ever' rang across the
grassy plains of the Curragh. The English boxer was plainly
upset at the crowd's partisanship just as he was at the fury of
their hero's attacks. The Dubliner again dominated the third
round and dealt out severe punishment with both hands.
Cooper went down to another burst of wild cheering.

The visitor showed his courage by fighting back so spirited-
ly in the fourth round that the home supporters were
momentarily silenced. He landed several solid thumps to
Donnelly's head. But when both men fell in a tangle to end
the round it was Cooper who was underneath. The betting
was now six to four on Donnelly.

The fifth was a good round for Cooper. He pounded
Donnelly about the head and then slipped neatly inside his
guard to hurl him heavily on his back with a mighty 'cross
buttock'. This particular tactic, though common in bare-
fist boxing, was more of a wrestling move. *Fistiana* described
it thus: 'When your sides come together you must manage to

get your arm firmly over your adversary's neck, grasping his loose arm with the other hand — then shifting yourself to his front, get his crutch upon your hip or buttock, give him a cant over your shoulder. If well done, the heels will go up in the air, he goes over with tremendous violence and you fall upon his abdomen. The chances are that he is either insensible or is so shaken by the fall that he loses all power of resisting your future attacks'.

Grose's Dictionary (1785) aptly explained the cross buttock as 'a particular lock or fall in the Broughtonian art which conveys more pleasurable sensations to the spectators than the patient'.

While Donnelly undoubtedly concurred with the latter's sentiment, he seemed not too badly shaken by the throw and regained his feet without the aid of his seconds. The odds were now even.

Cooper boxed quite brilliantly in the sixth round. His clever method of side-stepping the Irishman's crude rushes brought cheers even from the home supporters. Donnelly at last got to grips with his slippery rival and managed to wrestle him to the ground, but not without some difficulty.

The Irish champion, feeling the fight was going against him, came from his corner for the seventh round grimly determined to prove his greater strength would overcome his rival's superior science. He belted the retreating Cooper about the head with both hands.

Then, in a colossal display of might, he tossed the lighter man to the ground with what was described as 'one of the most dreadful cross buttocks ever witnessed'. For extra effect, he fell on Cooper with all his weight 'driving the wind nearly out of his body'.

'The Bargeman' never recovered from this shock. He appeared much distressed on toeing the line for the eighth round and Donnelly wasted no time in following up his advantage. He hammered Cooper without respite and knocked him off his feet with a fearful left-hander. Amid the tumultuous applause, a Donnelly supporter could be heard offering 'a guinea to a tenpenny bit' on his man.

The half-minute rest period seemed to refresh the gallant

Englishman to some extent and he held his own in some desperate close-range fighting in the ninth. Donnelly, over-anxious to end the bout, missed with a ponderous swipe and the momentum made him fall to the ground.

By the tenth round it was obvious that the Irish champion was much too strong for his rival, now fighting on reserves of courage alone. Donnelly had little trouble brushing aside his feeble attempts and countering with his own heavy punches. He tossed Cooper to end the round. Long odds were offered on Donnelly but there were no takers.

The eleventh round proved to be the last. Cooper, showing magnificent spirit, made a brief rally and scored with some stinging hits. Donnelly, however, took all he had to offer and finished the proceedings with two terrific smashes to knock the Englishman senseless. The last punch broke Cooper's jaw. The fight had lasted twenty-two minutes.

Incredible scenes of jubilation followed the Irish champion's triumph. Waves of cheering continued for several minutes as Dan, having provided words of condolence to his beaten opponent, struggled to make his way through the back-slapping crowd.

As he strode up the hill towards his carriage, fanatical followers dug out the imprints left by his feet. Known as 'The Steps to Strength and Fame', the footmarks are still to be seen in Donnelly's Hollow, leading from the monument which commemorates the scene of his greatest ring victory. Few of the summer picnickers who today frequent the historic spot could imagine the wild scenes that day a century and a half ago.

Rich men offered the hospitality of their homes to the conquering hero. Peasants fought among themselves for the chance to touch his brawny back and ladies waved dainty silk handkerchiefs from their coach windows in the hope that he would repay them with a smile. He did not disappoint them. A rewarding smile could be the prelude to more intimate contact when the immediate hubbub had died down.

Donnelly politely declined all the invitations to celebrate his triumph in the taverns of County Kildare. He had

*Donnelly's Hollow at the Curragh. To this day, over
a century and a half after his memorable victory over
England's George Cooper, the footprints of the Irish
champion, dug out by fanatical followers as he walked
from the ring and up the slope, are still clearly visible.
The monument, erected in 1888, commemorates
Donnelly's win over Cooper in December, 1815.*

promised his family and friends he would return to Dublin immediately after the fight.

And what a welcome he got in the capital. On arrival at Townsend Street, his coach was besieged by an ecstatic crowd who told him the celebrations had already begun and they begged him to join them at the Carlisle Tavern, opposite Carlisle Bridge (later reconstructed and re-named O'Connell Bridge). The festivities continued right through the night and Dan, after being called upon time and again to give his account of the fight to latecomers, joined heartily in the singing and several times danced to the tune of 'The Rakes of Kildare'.

Most extraordinary aspect of the celebrations, if we are to accept the account in the *Dublin Penny Journal,* must have been the part played by the champion's mother.

Recalling the event seventeen years later, in its issue of August 25, 1832, the newspaper gave this account: 'We remember well Donnelly's triumphal entry into Dublin after his great battle on the Curragh. That indeed was an ovation. He was borne on the shoulders of the people while his mother, like a Roman matron, leading the van in his procession and with all the pride of a second Agrippina, frequently slapped her naked bosom, exposed for the occasion, and exulting exclaimed: 'There's the breast that suckled him; there's the breast that suckled him'. Was the pride of a mother ever more admirably expressed!'

Quite a woman was Donnelly's mother. An even more enchanting story about her was that told to Anthony Raftery, the supposedly blind poet from County Mayo, by a former boxer from Galway named O'Donnell.

According to O'Donnell, Mrs. Donnelly once won a fiver by racing on foot against a horse over six miles — and winning by several lengths!

It seems that Dan was still at his mother's breast when his father one day met a member of a fox-hunt who boasted that he was the best horseman in the locality. Joseph Donnelly, so the story goes, retorted: 'Sure I know a woman, overburdened with a family, who could outpace you and your horse.'

The angry huntsman threatened he would have Donnelly run out of the country if he couldn't prove what he said. 'Well, I left her at home behind me,' said Donnelly, 'she's my wife and if she runs three miles of the road going and coming, that's six miles, and you trotting, without galloping, and she going as fast as she can and she can't beat you, then you may do what you want with me.'

The horseman said he would give him five pounds if he was right in what he said. Joseph went home and told his wife of the challenge and the brave Mrs. Donnelly, far from being put out, said: 'Oh, Joseph, it's a great supper we'll both be having tonight, seeing you wouldn't let him go full gallop.'

The couple immediately went to the horseman's house and the distance was arranged and the place where they would turn around. Mrs. Donnelly and the horse began the race and they were neck-and-neck at the turning point.

A quarter of a mile from home and the woman drew five yards ahead. She turned around to her rival and shouted: 'Are you not able to go any faster than that?' When she was one hundred and twenty yards ahead, he put the horse into full gallop but still Mrs. Donnelly finished first 'without being exhausted'. The horseman went straight into his house and handed Joseph Donnelly the five pounds. 'The gentleman had a great respect for Donnelly and his wife ever afterwards,' said the storyteller. 'He said they came of good stock.'

One Irishman who did not share the general enthusiasm after Donnelly's win over Cooper was the hotel proprietor in Robertstown, County Kildare, who had been told to prepare a 'victory banquet' for Cooper and his friends. The English boxer and his party had stayed at the hotel, Robertstown House, the night before the fight after travelling from Dublin by canal barge. So confident was Cooper that he ordered a celebration dinner for forty guests. After his defeat, the Englishman slipped quietly back to the city — this time by road — leaving an enraged hotelier with a kitchenful of unpaid-for food.

Meanwhile, the name of Dan Donnelly was earning respect

Robertstown House, by the Grand Canal in County Kildare, was booked for a 'victory banquet' by George Cooper before his fight with Donnelly. Cooper, a bargeman by trade, had travelled via the canal to the venue, but after his defeat he slipped quietly back to Dublin, by road. Opened in 1803, the hotel is still a popular banqueting spot, visitors still reaching it by boat.

among English boxing followers. Reports of his impressive win over Cooper won him the admiration of The Fancy, who had previously considered him as 'simply a big, clumsy rough'.

Boxiana noted that the Irish champion had 'shown improvement in both science and temper and was also in better condition than when he fought Hall. His superior strength enabled him to beat down the guard of Cooper with ease and effect'.

The Sporting Magazine commented: 'Since Donnelly fought Hall, we think there is no man could improve more than he has in fighting and if we may judge from his conduct this day, he has also improved in his temper. We venture to say that if he is to live regular and be advised by his friends, he would very soon be able to take the palm from the champion of England...'

Strength, determination, fitness — all had served to ensure victory for Donnelly over Cooper. Legend tells us there was another winning ingredient — a lump of sugar cane!

An enterprising Dublin character known as 'The Sugar Cane Man' did good business for many years through claiming that his merchandise was responsible for winning the fight for Donnelly at a point when all seemed lost. The story was told by P. J. McCall, treasurer of the original Library Association of Ireland, in a paper entitled *In the Shadow of St. Patrick's* which he read before the National Literary Society at their meeting on April 27, 1893, and which was later published in book form.

'The Sugar Cane Man', remembered McCall, came from Patrick Street, in the Liberties area of the city. A handsome little fellow with a drab coat and white apron, he carried the confectionery in a wooden tray suspended by a strap around his neck. In prose and verse, he would recite its magical properties. He attributed to the constant use of his sugar cane 'the pleasant expression to be seen on every true Irishman's face'.

He claimed that Donnelly was facing certain defeat in the fight with Cooper until Miss Kelly, Captain Kelly's sister, who had everything she possessed in the world staked on

Dan, waved her hand in front of him and, with a bewitching smile, gave him a packet containing two ounces of the sugar cane, whispering, 'Now, my charmer, give him a warmer'.

'The result', said the Sugar Cane Man, 'is a matter of history'.

Of the many street ballads that were written on the boxing ring, the most popular and enduring is undoubtedly that which commemorates Donnelly's victory over Cooper on the Curragh of Kildare.

Up to the early part of this century, when street ballads were still in vogue, the story of Dan's immortal triumph would hold a crowd spellbound while the singer, for the few pennies his listeners could spare, bellowed out the seemingly never-ending verses.

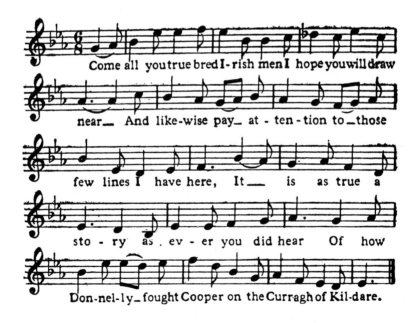

THE BALLAD OF DONNELLY AND COOPER

Come all you true bred Irishmen, I hope you will draw near,
    And likewise pay attention to these few lines I have here;
It is as true a story as ever you did hear
    Of how Donnelly fought Cooper on the Curragh of Kildare.

It was on the third of June, brave boys, the challenge was
    sent o'er
From Brittania to old Grania for to raise her son once more
    To renew the satisfaction and the credit to record,
They all in deep distraction since Daniel conquered all.

Old Grania read the challenge and received it with a smile,
    'You'd better haste unto Kildare, my well beloved child,
It is there you'll reign victorious as you often did before,
    And your deeds will shine most glorious around sweet
    Erin's shore.'

The challenge was accepted and those heroes did prepare
    To meet brave Captain Kelly on the Curragh of Kildare,
Those Englishmen bet ten to one that day against poor Dan,
    Such odds as these could ne'er dismay the blood of an
    Irishman.

When Donnelly and Cooper had stepped into the ring,
    'Shake hands,' says Dan to Cooper, 'before we do begin'.
From nine to six they parried on, till Donnelly knocked
    him down;
Old Grania cried, 'Well done, my child, that's worth ten
    thousand pounds'.

The second round that Cooper fought he knocked down
   Donnelly,
But Dan had steel, likewise true pluck, and rose most manfully;
    Right active then was Cooper and knocked Donnelly down
      once more;
The Englishmen, they all cried out, 'the battle he may give o'er'.

Long life unto Miss Kelly 'tis recorded on the plain,
    She boldly stepped into the ring saying 'Dan, what do you
      mean?'
Saying 'Dan, me boy, what do you mean? Hibernia's son,'
    says she,
'All my estate I have bet on you, brave Dan Donnelly.'

'Dan,' says she, 'that you're an Irishman the gentry all do know,
    'So on the Curragh of Kildare this day your valour show;
'Be sure you die before you fly, Hibernia's son,' says she,
    'My coach and horses I have bet on you, Dan Donnelly.'

Donnelly rose up again and meeting with great might,
    For to stagnate those nobles all, he continued with the fight;
Tho' Cooper stood in his own defence, exertion proved in vain,
    For he soon received a temple blow that hurled him o'er
      the rails.

You sons of proud Britannia, your boasting now recall,
    Since Cooper by Dan Donnelly has met his sad downfall;
In eleven rounds he got nine knockdowns, likewise a broke
    jaw-bone,
'Shake hands,' said she, 'brave Donnelly, the battle is all our
    own.'

Donnelly and Cooper provided the inspiration for many of the boxing ballads that followed. Like the unknown author of *Donnelly and Cooper,* the writers were deeply concerned with the glorification of Ireland's struggle against English domination, as symbolised when an Irish fist bloodied an English nose. There are several instances.

In *The Glorious Victory of Paddy Murphy, our Irish Champion, over Johnny Batts, the English Bully, at Moyvalley,* the ballad writer, P. J. Fitzpatrick, tells how Murphy draws new strength from remembering Donnelly's famous triumphs.

Remember Daniel Donnelly in days that are gone by,
He beat three English champions and their science did defy,
The Prince of Wales asked Donnelly, are you old Ireland's
    boast
Said valiant Dan I'm the best man upon your English coast.

After Batts, the Englishman, is battered to the ground and 'lay there with many a wound and sore,' the ballad writer gives him this parting advice:

Now Johnny Batts take my advice and quick as ere you
    can,
To grope your way or get a guide and leave this Irish land,
And tell John Bull when you go home in future to beware,
To never fight an Irishman again in sweet Kildare.

In another ballad, *Heenan, the Bold Benicia Boy,* an Irish-American heavyweight named John C. Heenan (his father was an emigrant from Dun Laoghaire, then called Kingstown) does a fair impression of a 19th century Muhammad Ali when he predicts of his forthcoming fight with the Englishman Tom Sayers:

I can lick him like a gander at any time I choose,

I can knock his very eyeballs from his forehead to
 his shoes.

Brave Donnelly was an Irishman who did for no man care,

Just as he walloped Cooper, I mean to beat Tom Sayers.

Unfortunately for Heenan, Sayers stoutly defied his best efforts and the best he could achieve was a draw.

Heenan fell out of favour with the Irish when he was alleged to have 'sold' a fight against Tom King, an Englishman, in 1862. Animosity was heightened when it was suggested that the 'Benicia Boy' did not support the cause of nationalism.

The bitterness towards Heenan is clear in this extract from a ballad called *Coburn's Challenge to Heenan*. Joe Coburn, from Armagh, asserts his dislike in taking on a 'fellow Irishman' but demands satisfaction by beating the 'traitor'.

Heenan my boy get ready and do not flinch from me

I'll show you the way that Cooper fell by Daniel Donnelly

Money will not buy me for gold I do not care

I'll fight in defence of Paddy's land and the laurel that
 I wear.

Heenan must not have been too concerned as to what Coburn, or the Irish, thought of him, for he turned a deaf ear to Coburn's challenge. Coburn, who had quite a feared reputation, then accused Jem Mace, the English champion, of running away from a proposed match.

In the ballad entitled *The Cowardly Englishman*, Dan Donnelly is recalled yet again as the model for Irish ring heroes. One verse goes as follows:

Our champion (Coburn) in great courage with his seconds
faced the ring,
But Mace the cowardly bully to his fight they could not
bring,
I'm sure he thought of Cooper when his jaw was broke
in two,
For Granua's sons were never beat in all that they went
through.

Another Irish fighter whose blood was stirred by the gallant exploits of Donnelly was John Morrisey, born in Tipperary in 1831, who on his retirement from the ring made a fortune from running luxurious gambling houses in New York. He became a prominent figure in politics there, serving two terms in Congress and was elected to the State Senate in 1877.

In the ballad, *The great victory of John Morrisey over the Russian Sailor Boy* (fought in Terra del Fuego, South America, for 60,000 dollars), the Tipperary man, five inches shorter and four stone lighter, batters his opponent so severely in 38 rounds that the doctors said the Russian would never fight again. The penultimate verse of the ballad goes:

Our hero conquer'd Thompson and the Yankee
Clipper too
The Benecia Boy and Shepherd he so nobly did subdue
Unto our bold Tipperary Boy the Russian forced to yield
Brave Morrisey like Donnelly would die or gain the field.

AN'S PURSE MONEY of £60 from the Cooper fight lasted for five weeks. Then it was back to work in the carpenter's shop. The reception he got from his employer in no way matched that accorded him by his adoring followers. Indeed, he was told bluntly that he had better take his job more seriously or he would soon be looking for alternative employment.

A short time later, a wealthy Dublin timber merchant who was one of Donnelly's staunchest admirers made an attractive offer to the discontented carpenter. He would set him up as a publican if Dan would give a firm promise to work hard and endeavour to make the business a success. Donnelly was delighted to accept.

Evidence that the consumption of alcohol was then, even more than today, the favourite pastime of the Irish masses was the fact that, in 1804, there were no less than fifty-five breweries and twenty-five distilleries located in the Dublin area alone. A census conducted some fifty years earlier showed that the Irish capital had the grand total of two thousand ale houses, three hundred taverns and twelve hundred brandy shops. Many writers of the period condemned the excessive drinking of whiskey and called it a great national evil. The wretchedness of the social conditions was largely blamed for the population seeking its 'escape' in alcohol.

Then, as now, it was common to find boxer-publicans. Many wellknown English pugilists, among them Tom Cribb, Tom Spring, Jack Randall, Ben Burns, 'Gentleman' John Jackson, Bill Richmond and Joe Ward, all ran taverns at one time or another. Bob Gregson held the licence of the Castle Tavern, in Holborn, London, under the name of 'Bob's Chop House', before coming to Ireland to run a public house in Moore Street, Dublin. Another English prizefighter, Tom Johnson, lost the licence of a Dublin premises 'from his house not proving so consonant to the principles of propriety as were wished'.

It was generally considered good business sense for a popular boxer to run a pub. His fame would entice extra customers eager to be entertained by stirring tales of the prizering. Whether such a move was to the pugilist's benefit was open to doubt. As one contemporary writer stated: 'The landlord must drink with his friends or else be a churl... and should he again enter the ring he gives the chance away of two points out of three against himself'.

To emphasise his misgivings, the writer noted the danger that the publican, 'in serving others plentifully with this luscious liquid, he would serve himself so often and so copiously'.

Donnelly's public house in Capel Street, Dublin, was an instant success and the new licensee, to his credit, worked hard at his new occupation. On opening night, the timber merchant who had set him up presented him with a quantity of wine, spirits and porter to the value of £150, a considerable sum for that time. The Irish champion proved a major attraction and the crowds flocked to his premises. Trade was so brisk in the first three months, it was said, that the waiters had no time for meal breaks.

Dan felt like a man reborn. He married the girl he had been courting for some time and seemed ready and willing to meet his responsibilities as a husband and businessman. His aged mother left her Townsend Street home and went to live with Dan in Capel Street. She took charge of the tavern kitchen, while Dan's wife helped run the bar.

As for boxing, the Irish champion showed no great desire to re-enter the prizering. Apart from taking part in occasional exhibition matches on benefit tournaments for down-and-out fighters, he gave all his energy and attention to running the tavern.

The realisation that Donnelly might have retired from the ring brought dejection to his faithful followers. In England, too, The Fancy were disappointed that they were not to see for themselves if the Irishman lived up to his reputation. George Cooper had, on his return home after his defeat by Donnelly, suggested that there was no one to equal Dan among the English pugilists. It was strongly rumoured that Cooper, as a result of the beating he had taken, was disabled and confined to his room in London. *The Sporting Magazine* of December, 1815, even reported Cooper's 'death' a few weeks after the fight, supposedly from the tremendous blows he received on that occasion. Though unfounded, the reports served to add to Donnelly's reputation as 'a formidable buffer'.

Pierce Egan, editor of *Boxiana* and probably the number one boxing expert of his time, said of Donnelly: 'He is in possession of every requisite to constitute a first-rate boxer. He is in height about six feet, weighing 14 stone, gifted with prodigious strength, no lack of courage, a good knowledge of the science and backed with the prime advantage of youth, being under 30 years of age. The blows of Donnelly are described as terrific and appalling and in their operation more like the ponderosity of a sledgehammer than given from the arm of a human being, added to which he has a peculiar sort of hitch, or fastening, that gives him great facility in cross-buttocking his opponents when in the act of closing. He has an animated countenance and his head altogether portrays a staunch milling index'.

Repeated efforts were made to entice the Irish champion back to the ring, but to no avail. The Fancy, however, were not ready to admit defeat.

Inevitably, after the initial excitement of his new life began to pall, Donnelly drifted back to his irresponsible ways. Business and family considerations took second place to regular drinking sessions with his cronies. Often he would not appear at the public house for days, leaving the running of the business to his over-worked wife. Many customers took advantage of the landlord's absence to slip away without paying for the drink they consumed. Mrs. Donnelly was either too busy to notice them or physically incapable of stopping them.

When Dan sobered up for long enough to be told that he was tossing away a lucrative living, he took heed and settled down — for a short while. He soon lost interest again and, hardly surprisingly, those regulars who had thronged his premises to talk to their idol now began to drift away. If the main attraction did not put in an appearance, who could expect an audience?

Donnelly finally came to his senses — but it was too late to save the ailing business. He had run up heavy debts during his latest wild drinking spree and yielded to the temptation to return to boxing as a way of making up his losses.

He went back into light training while efforts were made to find one of the top English pugilists willing to come to Ireland to meet him. There was no rush of volunteers. It is likely that his fighting reputation, allied to reports that one could not be assured of a fair deal in fighting the Irishman on his own soil, frightened off prospective opponents. Tom Hall had insisted he was cheated of victory when Donnelly hit him while he was down. George Cooper, apart from not receiving his agreed purse, said the Irish fans were prepared to go to any lengths to help their man win. One of his seconds, Ned Painter, had been hit by a stone thrown into the ring by the partisan crowd.

It was clear that if he wanted a fight, Donnelly would have to go to England. This he was not prepared to do.

He decided to have another try at being a publican, this time taking the licence of premises in the Liberties area of Dublin on the corner of The Coombe and New Row. This is 'The Capstan Bar', remarkably still in business under the name of John Fallon and Sons.

During the spell Donnelly pulled pints there, he lived across the road at the corner of Francis Street. He was an extremely popular figure with the locals of the Liberties. Among the knights of the steel and cleaver, or 'The Bull Alley Yeomen', as they were known, Dan was revered as a demi-god, wrote P. J. McCall.

Once again, however, the incorrigible Irishman lost a glorious opportunity to keep a profitable trade going. He fell back into his old habits and lost whatever financial gains he had made. In yet another attempt to make good as a licensee, he ran a public house in Poolbeg Street, in the dockland area where he had grown up. But he was too well known there and was not a great attraction. Also, he was far too liberal with free drinks for his old buddies. He soon fell into heavy debt once more.

After a heart-to-heart talk with his family and close

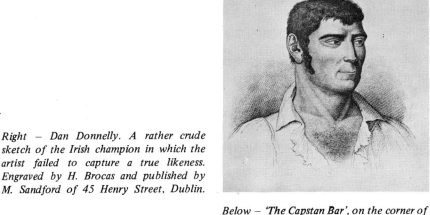

Right – Dan Donnelly. A rather crude sketch of the Irish champion in which the artist failed to capture a true likeness. Engraved by H. Brocas and published by M. Sandford of 45 Henry Street, Dublin.

Below – 'The Capstan Bar', on the corner of The Coombe and New Row, in the Liberties area of Dublin, which was the second of four public houses run by Dan Donnelly. The others were in Capel Street, Poolbeg Street and at the corner of Greek Street and Pill Lane. It was on the latter premises that Donnelly took ill and died.

friends, Dan decided there was only one course open to him. He would have to go to England. His aim was not to fight in the prizering, but merely to pick up the ready cash available for boxing exhibitions. This would enable him to pay off whatever debts there were and to make a sincere attempt to make good as a publican.

He got in touch with Jack Carter, reckoned by many to be the top heavyweight in England, whom Dan had first met when Carter seconded Tom Hall in the fight against him. Carter readily accepted the Irish champion's suggestion that a series of sparring matches would be a big attraction in Britain.

The English Fancy would relish the chance to see for themselves what the highly-lauded Irish champion was made of.

Dan bid a somewhat reluctant farewell to his family and friends and set sail on the packet steamer from Ringsend to Liverpool. The monotony of the eighteen hours at sea was relieved by 'a few glasses of whiskey and a sound forty winks'.

By prior arrangement, he was met on arrival by an Irish-born innkeeper called Regan, who was so great a fan of the boxer that he offered him free lodgings for as long as he stayed in Liverpool. The hospitality lavished upon Donnelly by the Liverpool Irish was hardly conducive to his keeping in good physical condition for the proposed boxing programme. His landlord, Regan, threw regular all-night parties during Dan's stay with him.

Donnelly made no attempt to keep control of himself. Indeed, he revelled in his new-found freedom. He lost no time in proving his charm with the opposite sex, although he would invariably regret his giving in to 'the temptations of the flesh', blaming it on the demon drink. It was obvious that heavy drinking, while accounting for some boxers becoming more aggressive, had the effect on Donnelly of making him more amorous.

An unsavoury incident on the night before he left Liverpool for Manchester, where he had arranged to meet Jack Carter, typified his shameless behaviour. Regan lent his tavern to a riotous farewell party for the departing champion. Long after midnight, the host was fast asleep in an armchair while Donnelly lay half-draped across a table. His senses were not sufficiently dulled as to fail to notice a pretty young maid smiling in his direction. He thought it strange that he had not noticed her up to that time. The girl approached him.

'Mr. Donnelly,' she said, 'you do look tired. Let me help you to your room'.

Dan mumbled his gratitude and placed his arm around the girl's slim shoulders as she helped him climb the two flights of stairs. They entered his room together and the girl gently closed the door behind them.

A few hours later, the landlord's throbbing head was in no way relieved by the thumping of a heavy fist upon his bedroom door accompanied by the enraged shouts of the Irish champion.

'What's the matter, Dan?' groaned Regan.

'Where is my money and my clothes,' yelled his honoured guest. 'I must meet Carter in Manchester in a few hours and all I can find are my shirt and pants'.

Regan was perplexed. Together, the two men searched the house from top to bottom. There was no sign of the missing items. It was only when Donnelly told his host of the girl who accompanied him to his room that the truth dawned on Regan. He did not have a maid fitting the description Dan gave him. Obviously, the girl was an unscrupulous type who had slipped into the tavern when everyone was too drunk to notice her and, posing as a maid, had chosen her all-too-willing victim. Donnelly, cursing his stupidity, was more worried about the loss of his clothes than anything else.

A local tailor was summoned and, luckily, he had a suit to fit Dan. Regan met the cost and also gave his friend enough money to tide him over his initial spell in Manchester.

THE FOLLOWING notice went on display in Manchester: 'Donnelly, Champion of Ireland, and Carter, Champion of England, will exhibit together in various combats the art of self-defence at the Emporium Rooms on February 18, 1819.'

While Donnelly's right to be called his country's champion was undisputed, it was taking something of a liberty to bill Carter as the English titleholder. That honour was still claimed by Tom Cribb, even though he had not fought for almost eight years.

Carter, known as 'The Lancashire Hero', was a good, scientific boxer with a punishing left hand — he used his right sparingly — and was certainly one of his country's top fighting men. But he was found somewhat lacking in staying power.

Though he held victories over redoubtable foes like George Cooper and Tom Oliver, he did not distinguish himself in his fight with the black man, Tom Molyneux. He collapsed on his second's knee when a win was within his grasp. A canal navigator by trade, Carter was credited with other talents besides prizefighting. He won twelve out of fourteen walking and running races. A good dancer, 'he performed the clog hornpipe with considerable ability'. And it was claimed that he could drink several pints of ale while standing on his head!

His successful boxing partnership with Donnelly was, sadly, to end in a bitter, prolonged row which earned little credit for Carter, even among his fellow countrymen.

Whether the Manchester fans accepted Carter's aspirations to the championship of England or not, the first exhibition match with Donnelly proved a great attraction. Many were turned away at the doors of the packed Emporium Rooms. It was the same success story in Liverpool and the other major boxing centres where the pair appeared.

Donnelly's fighting ability impressed The Fancy, who were ready to concede that the Irish might have a man capable of matching the best men in England. *Boxiana* observed: 'The Irish champion is an acknowledged first-rate boxer and from the repeated use of the gloves he has derived great improvement. The size, strength and science of Donnelly qualify him to fight any man in the world'.

But the sceptical Londoners were yet to see Donnelly perform. Growing demand for him to appear in the metropolis forced Dan to overcome his earlier reluctance. He knew only too well the temptations the big city had to offer would be hard to resist. But that was where the real money could be earned from sparring matches so he and Carter headed for London.

The London fans and especially the Irish immigrants turned out in force to see Donnelly's debut in the capital at the Peacock Theatre, Gray's Inn Road, on March 18. They were well pleased with what they saw. Donnelly's greater strength and powerful hitting were balanced by the more scientific, agile style of Carter.

'The difference in styles was most marked,' reported Pierce Egan in *Boxiana,* 'Carter an agile, confident dancing master, walking round and round, picking his blows with the perfection of a professor. Donnelly is not so showy but he is dangerous. He is no tapper, nor does he throw his blows away. He makes tremendous use of the right hand. Nor is he to be got at without encountering mischief. He is, however, awkward. His attitude (sparring pose) was not admired and it was thought he leaned too far back, inclining to his right shoulder. But final judgement cannot be pronounced from sparring, more especially as Donnelly does not profess use of the gloves. It was a close affair with honours about even'.

The following Thursday, Donnelly appeared at the Minor Theatre, in Catherine Street, off The Strand. A new sparmate, Ben Burns, a boxer of considerable class, exposed the visitor's scientific limitations. Dan's habit of standing too far back and leaning away make it difficult for him to counter-punch quickly, but he was dangerous at all times and this made the contest interesting. The set-to was loudly applauded. Dan finished the night's entertainment with a sharp few rounds against Carter.

Supporters of the Irish champion, while conceding that he did not show up too well in gloved sparring sessions, boasted that in a genuine barefist battle to the finish no prizefighter in England could match him.

The call went out for the supreme test — a meeting with Tom Cribb, the champion of England. That such a contest never took place is a great pity. The Irishman's detractors have long held that, because he never fought top-rated contemporaries like Cribb and Tom Spring, his true worth was much exaggerated by the fanciful Irish. While this might have been true, there is no denying that Donnelly's renowned strength, powerful punching and great potential made him a good bet against anyone else in the world at that time.

Had the match with Cribb been arranged, it is likely that Donnelly would have emerged victorious after a long, bruising battle. His great endurance and refusal to concede defeat would surely have overcome Cribb, then thirty-eight, who had not fought since his second gruelling win over Tom Molyneux eight years earlier.

And Tom Spring, Cribb's successor as English titleholder, while a better stylist than Donnelly, was not nearly as heavy a hitter. Spring suffered from brittle hands which caused him to be called some unflattering names, like 'The Lady's Maid' and 'The Powder-puff Fighter'. This weakness might have proved costly in a prolonged set-to with the Irish champion.

The growing demand for a contest between the champions of England and Ireland seemed answered to some extent when it was announced that Cribb and Donnelly would box at the Minor Theatre on a charity tournament for Bob Gregson. It would, of course, be merely an exhibition with both contestants wearing gloves. But it would at least give some indication of how the two men shaped in opposition.

The date, April 1, 1819, proved significant. It was an April Fool's hoax. Donnelly appeared as scheduled but there was no sign of the English champion. The packed crowd understandably voiced their anger and their mood grew even uglier when it was stated that Donnelly could not box as he had injured his arm in falling off the Oxford stagecoach.

Fearing a riot, the promoters pleaded with Dan to put on the gloves and spar a few rounds with Jack Carter. Donnelly agreed and the crowd was pacified — but only for a short

Left – Tom Cribb, one of the most celebrated of England's champions. His reign lasted from 1809 until his retirement in 1822. Efforts to match him with Dan Donnelly proved fruitless and even several scheduled exhibition matches between the champions of England and Ireland did not materialise.

Below – Prizefighting often took as heavy a toll on the winner as the loser in prolonged encounters. Here, English champion Tom Cribb's right eye is swollen shut as he batters the black American, Tom Molyneux, in 1811.

ONE OF THE BATTLE or the CHAMPION TRIUMPHANT.

while.

It was soon clear that Donnelly, unable to block punches with his badly bruised and swollen right arm, could not go on for long. Carter did not wish to add to his sparmate's discomfort and, as a result, few blows were attempted by either man before the affair was halted. Loud booing followed the contestants as they left the stage.

A member of the audience, Harry Sutton, one of several American-born negroes who had come to England in search of ring fame, was so encouraged by the tame showing of Donnelly that he stepped onto the stage to publicly challenge him to a match for £50-a-side.

The crowd, now clearly against the Irishman, called on him to accept the challenge. Bill Richmond entered the ring on Donnelly's behalf and said that Dan 'did not come to England with any intention of entering the prizering'. The statement was greeted with a storm of booing and abuse directed at Donnelly.

Donnelly could be seen whispering to Carter and the latter then announced that Dan would consult his friends in Ireland and England about the possibility of fighting Sutton. Roars of derisory laughter came from the audience.

Sutton again entered the ring and, to tremendous cheers, stated that he would fight Donnelly for £50 at five minutes' notice, or for £100 or £200 at any given time.

Dan was so upset by the insinuations of cowardice cast by the crowd that he had the following notice published in the London newspapers for a few days later: 'At a sparring match for the benefit of Gregson, on Thursday the first day of April, Donnelly, having met with an accident, hopes the public will pardon him if he has not amused the gentlemen present to their satisfaction. After the set-to between Harmer and Sutton, the latter thought proper to come forward and challenge any men, and Donnelly in particular, for £50, £100 or £200.

'Donnelly, being something of a stranger, did not come forward to answer the challenge until he should first consult his friends in this country and in Ireland, but he has confidence that his friends will back him. He therefore begs

Standing room only was the order of the day at popular London venues like the Fives Court, in Little St. Martin's Street, off The Strand, when top pugilists (including Dan Donnelly) took part in sparring matches with the gloves. The Fancy, as followers of the sport were known, recognised no race, class or age barriers, as this painting of the scene at the exhibition between Jack Randall and Ned Turner shows. Even a dog (bottom left) managed to make itself at home. It was at the Fives Court that the challenge was thrown out to Donnelly for a fight with Tom Oliver, which the Irish champion accepted.

leave to say that he did not come to England for the purpose of fighting, but it appears to be the wish of the gentlemen here to try his mettle. He begs leave further to say that he will fight any man in England of his weight for £100 to £500.'

No more was heard of Sutton's desire to fight him and, while awaiting replies to his open challenge, Donnelly continued to box exhibitions. But his standing with the English Fancy had taken a considerable plunge. It did not help his esteem when another publicised sparring bout against Cribb, at the Fives Court, in Little St. Martin's Street, on April 6, again failed to come off.

As Donnelly and Carter entered the ring that evening, there was a loud chant of 'Cribb, Cribb, Cribb'. The upset Irish champion threatened to withdraw from the exhibition, but it was Carter, even angrier at the crowd's reception, who stormed out of the ring.

The audience became somewhat subdued when they realised that there might be no show and they called for Carter to return. But the 'Lancashire Hero', his pride hurt, had in a fit of temper already left the hall. In the midst of the confusion, Harry Harmer offered to spar with Donnelly.

Plainly disconcerted by the hostile reception and still suffering discomfort from his injured arm, Dan boxed well below his true form and Harmer had much the better of the exchanges. The Irishman wore a pained expression as he left the ring to hissing and booing.

Pierce Egan, in *Boxiana,* criticised the London crowd's treatment of Donnelly. 'It was very unlike the usual generosity of John Bull towards a stranger. It was not national but savoured something like prejudice. Such partialities ought not to be exhibited'.

There was only one way Donnelly could win the respect of the London Fancy — by taking part in a real prizefight and defeating one of England's top men. It was to the delight of all boxing fans when it was announced that Dan had accepted a challenge from Tom Oliver for a match for a hundred guineas-a-side. The challenge had been made by Oliver during a benefit tournament for Sam Martin at the Fives

Court. Donnelly was not present so Jack Randall accepted on his behalf.

Donnelly, determined to show the English he was every bit as good as his fellow-countrymen said he was, gave his most impressive display to date in an exhibition bout with Jack Carter at the Minor Theatre on April 27. He cleverly blocked most of the Englishman's best punches and took the grin off Carter's face with some stinging right-handers.

Carter was training to fight Tom Spring at Crawley Downs in Sussex, on May 4, and may have been more intent on keeping out of mischief than fully exerting himself. Nevertheless there was much praise for Donnelly's improved showing.

Dan sadly saw his regular sparmate going down to defeat against Spring after one hour and fifty-five minutes of hard battling and afterwards he asked the winner if he would consent to meeting him in an exhibition. Spring was happy to oblige and the bout was fixed for the Minor Theatre on May 25.

Donnelly, awaiting final arrangements to be made for the fight against Oliver, was at the peak of his form in the sparring match against Spring. He blocked many of Spring's best blows with admirable skill and his alertness in skipping away and returning to the attack drew loud applause.

Though only an exhibition, this was a performance of considerable merit by the Irishman. Spring, whose real name in fact was Winter, was reckoned one of the most skilled ringmen of his era, despite his brittle hands. He has since been described as 'the James J. Corbett of his time', a tribute to his speed, grace and scientific boxing. He was beaten only once — by Ned Painter — in his ten-year career, took the championship of England on Tom Cribb's retirement in 1821 and himself retired after twice defeating Irishman Jack Langan in lengthy duels in 1824.

Donnelly's ability to shine in his encounter with Spring led to the observation that he had either acquired considerable skill since his arrival in England or he had been hiding his true talents.

Final details of the proposed fight against Tom Oliver

were worked out when the boxers and their backers met at Dignam's tavern, The Red Lion in Haughton Street, Clare Market. One of Donnelly's patrons was a well known General in sporting circles who, shortly after Dan's arrival in England, personally tested the visitor's ability. After being sent reeling from a fierce blow to the face, the General was convinced Dan was well worthy of his support.

Tom Spring (real name Thomas Winter) who reigned as English heavyweight champion from 1821 to his retirement after twice beating Irishman Jack Langan in 1824. Six feet tall, he was a skilled boxer though not regarded as a heavy puncher. Although he boxed Donnelly in an exhibition in London in May 1819, the pair never met in a fight to the finish, as their respective fans had hoped.

WHEELER'S, A POPULAR training camp for pugilists at Riddlesdown, three miles from Croydon in Surrey, was chosen for Donnelly's preparation for the Oliver fight. It is a source of amazement and some amusement to modern boxers, who spend many weeks of varied, strenuous work in preparing for a contest, to learn of the simple methods of training for bare-knuckle combat. Great emphasis was laid upon long walks and some sprinting, necessary to build up stamina for long, exhausting contests. Apart from some sparring practice, light exercises and 'the avoidance of excesses, either in food, wine or women', little else was considered necessary.

A good example of how the early 19th century boxer was expected to train for a fight was the following advice given by *Fistiana:* 'Each day rise with the sun. Wash. Trot (the extreme pace of toe and heel) for one mile to three. Eat a dry biscuit. Run home. Have breakfast, lasting ten to fifteen minutes and consisting of boiled mutton or beef and potatoes. Rub down, lasting half an hour, and then walk until about eleven o'clock, during which one to three miles should be run at top speed. A rest to talk to patron and, at 12 noon, a sparring bout lasting about an hour and imitating in earnestness and length the prospective fight. About two o'clock have dinner, lasting not more than an hour and consisting of the same diet. Then more walking exercise and to bed with the sun'.

It was Captain Barclay, Donnelly's trainer, who first drew the attention of the boxing world to the inestimable value of correct preparation. His most acclaimed feat was in reducing the weight of Tom Cribb who 'from his mode of living in London and the confinement of a crowded city, had become corpulent, big-bellied, full of gross humours and short-breathed', from 16 stone to 13 stone 5 lbs. in nine weeks.

Barclay was a great believer in the regular movement of the bowels and prescribed frequent doses of physic. As for food and drink, he insisted that 'veal and lamb should never be given, nor vegetables such as turnips, carrots or potatoes, as they are watery and difficult to digest. Neither butter or cheese is allowed. Eggs are also forbidden, except the yolk taken raw in the morning. Liquors must always be taken cold and home-brewed beer, old but not bottled, is the best. Water must never be given and ardent spirits are strictly prohibited, however diluted'.

Barclay was adamant on one other point: 'The sexual intercourse must vanish and be no more heard of within the first week of training'.

Whereas Cribb obviously thrived on Barclay's strict regimen, as did Barclay himself, there is little doubt that Donnelly found the exacting course too regimental for his liking. Dan was so convinced that excess of any kind would not hurt him that he acted as he pleased.

And Donnelly was addicted to two of the things that Barclay forbade for a boxer in training – women and drink.

Dan's own opinion on how a pugilist should prepare for a bout is something of a classic in its own right. When asked by Jack Langan how he should spend the night before an important contest, Donnelly advised the young Irish heavyweight: 'First take off your shirt. Then walk up and down the room briskly and hit out well with both hands. Jump backwards and forwards at least 100 times. As it is now midnight, go home directly, drink half a gallon of the sourest buttermilk you can find and go to bed. At five o'clock in the morning, not a minute later, you must get up and run three or four miles. And at every mile you must swig – not whiskey, mind you – but a quart of spring water'.

Langan, following his idol's instructions faithfully, had only a few hours' sleep before rising at dawn. After knocking up all the dairymen in the neighbourhood, all he could get was three pints of buttermilk. To make up for this deficiency, he drank a greater quantity of water.

Considering the extremes Langan had gone to, it is not surprising that he was half an hour late for the fight. His opponent was just leaving the ring, in fact, when he arrived. Langan had a tough time in the early rounds before finally subduing his rival after 35 minutes. It is a matter of conjecture whether Donnelly's tuition had aided his ability to win or had prevented him scoring a quicker victory.

But then Donnelly was hardly the best man from whom to seek advice on training. To him, the task of getting down to even a half-strict routine was a bore. He longed for the day of the fight when it would be over and done with. It was usual for a prizefighter to have a close companion to see that he observed the training programme, but in Donnelly's case no one could keep the reins on him.

The Irish champion's most constant companion at Riddlesdown before the Oliver fight was a bottle of whiskey. He even took it to bed with him. He claimed he needed 'a small drop of stuff to make me sleep'.

'At other times,' disclosed *Boxiana*, 'he stole out in the dark like a poacher to procure 'game' — and the preserves of Croydon supplied more than his wants'. It hardly needs explaining that the 'game' he bagged were not birds of the feathered variety!'

Dan took nobody's advice but his own. He would make a joke of anyone's suggestion that his training methods were, to say the least, unorthodox.

On one occasion at Riddlesdown, when he was helping himself to large quantities of green peas at dinner, a member of the company remarked that peas were hard to digest and therefore unsuitable for a boxer preparing for a contest. Donnelly burst into a fit of laughter.

'Sure a few peas won't harm me, no more than a drop of the cratur,' he said. 'And now I'll show you how I'll take the peas and the liquor out of me'. With that, he left the table and immediately ran up the steep hill in front of Wheeler's house, returning a few minutes later in a state of perspiration, still grinning broadly.

All things considered, the Irish champion looked in remarkably good condition on the day of the fight. Pierce Egan described him thus in *Boxiana*: 'On stripping, Donnelly exhibited as fine a picture of a human frame as can be imagined. His legs were firm and well-rounded, his arms slingy and powerful. The tout ensemble indicated prodigious strength'.

Tom Oliver, who had trained diligently for the fight, was said to be in the best condition of his career. 'His flesh was as firm as a rock' noted Egan.

In Donnelly's case, his appearance was deceptive. Both during the fight and afterwards it was clear that he was in far from top condition and that he was paying the price of his wild ways.

A nobleman who backed Oliver called upon Donnelly the day before the fight and attempted to undermine the Irishman's confidence by remarking: 'About this time tomorrow you can expect a pretty head from the fists of Oliver'. Dan looked him straight in the face and replied: 'I was not born in a wood to be scared by an owl'. The nobleman said he would bet £15 to £10 on Oliver, which Donnelly gladly accepted.

THE RAIN FELL in torrents on the Wednesday morning of July 21, 1819. To add to the discomfort of those who arrived early at Bledlow Common, in Buckinghamshire, they were told that the venue for the fight had been switched to Crawley Downs, in Sussex, sixty-two miles away.

The reason for the last-minute change of location was for fear of intervention by the law. Prizefighting was at that time illegal, not because of its brutality, as might be imagined, but rather because a number of boxers were known to have 'sold' fights, thus causing it to be labelled a crooked sport. In spite of the ban, which lasted until 1901, prizefights were regularly held, usually in places where the local magistrates and police were sympathetic enough to turn a blind eye to the proceedings.

The realisation that the Donnelly v Oliver fight would not be held at Bledlow was a particularly sad blow to the hundreds of youngsters who had been up at the crack of dawn to make the journey in the steady downpour and climb the trees to secure 'roosting places' overlooking the site. Few of them could now face the long extra trip to Crawley Downs.

The contest had generated great excitement among the Fancy both in Britain and Ireland. Many of Donnelly's supporters made the journey across the Irish Sea to witness their hero's first prizefight on English soil. This time even the English were not convinced that their man would be able to turn back the Irish challenge. Donnelly was seven-to-one on favourite.

And the betting was not merely on the result, but on who would gain 'first blood', or if either man would win within half an hour or an hour, or if Oliver would prove the favourite at any stage during the battle. An estimated £100,000 was said to have been laid out in wagers, a staggering sum for that time, if true.

Prizefight attendance was a great social leveller in an age of wide class divisions. Although the Fancy was mainly composed of the lower orders, it had its share of 'gentlemen'

SPARRING, *Dedicated to the Fancy.*

The Fancy, over their beer and 'baccy, enjoying a sparring match between two unknown pugilists. On the wall behind the seated fans are sketches of famed boxers. This drawing, thought to be by George Cruikshank, was made in early 19th century.

too. 'Around a prize ring,' wrote Pierce Egan, 'every greasy hero or sooty chief placed himself by the side of the swells without any apology as feeling he had the right to do so. Selection is entirely out of the question.. the noble lord and the needy commoner are both at home after they have paid their tip for admission'.

The Fancy is usually considered to mean the followers of pugilism, the fighters, the patrons, the trainers, the crowds, all those whose 'fancy' was the prize ring. But Egan and other contemporary writers insist that the term did not restrict The Fancy to followers of boxing, but embraced other fancied sports such as cock fighting, dog fighting and bear and badger baiting.

William Hazlitt accused the Fancy of having no imagination, of restricting their topics of conversation to fighting men and dogs, to bears and badgers. Another writer remarked that they scarcely ever opened their mouths without finishing the sentences with 'I'll bet you two-to-one or six-to-four'.

But when the Fancy assembled at a fight, all men were equal. The Duke of Clarence, later King William IV, is said to have been at a fight at Moulsey Hurst when he saw a noble-man looking with distaste at the crowd. The Duke scolded him: 'Be pleased to recollect, my lord, that we are all Englishmen here'.

Egan's *Life in London* describes the surprise felt by the countryman, Jerry, when he visits the Royal Cockpit at Tufton Street, London, and finds 'flue-fakers (chimney sweeps), dustmen, lamp-lighters, stagecoachmen, bakers, farmers, barristers, swells, butchers, dog-fanciers, grooms, donkey-boys, weavers, snobs, market-men, watermen, honourables, sprigs of the nobility, M.P.s, mailguards, swaddies, etc., all in rude contact, jostling and pushing against each other, when the doors were opened to procure a front seat'.

Tom, the Corinthian, explains to his country cousin, Jerry: 'They are all sporting characters and are all touched more or less with the scene before them; and the flue-faker will drop his bender (sixpence) with as much pluck as the Honourable does his fifty, to support his opinion. The spirit is the same and it is only the blunt (money) that makes the difference'.

Oliver was the first of the contestants to arrive at Crawley Downs, at 1.30 p.m. He tossed his hat into the ring as a sign that he was ready to do battle. He was seconded by Tom Cribb and Tom Shelton, while the noble lord who was his patron stayed in close attendance.

Donnelly made his way to the ring to loud cheers from his fellow countrymen. 'Success to you, Dan', they shouted, and 'Ireland for ever'.

Both men stripped and tied their coloured silk handkerchiefs to one of the wooden stakes that held up the ropes. The green silk for Ireland was placed over the blue for England. It was customary for the winner to take both silks. Oliver's striped silk stockings drew much attention and comment.

Donnelly was attended in his corner by Tom Belcher and Jack Randall. In those days, the seconds actually stayed in the ring throughout the contest. One was known as 'the bottle man' because he carried the inter-round refreshment. The other was 'the knee man', whose job at the end of each round was to go down on one knee with the other leg providing a seat for his boxer.

Donnelly's opponent was more renowned for his great courage than for his boxing skill or punching power. But Oliver was considerably more experienced than the Irishman and numbered among his victims Ned Painter (whom he beat twice), Ned Hopping, Harry Lancaster, William Ford and Black Kendrick. He had also defeated Donnelly's last opponent, George Cooper, in seventeen minutes. It was Oliver's losing battles with Jack Carter and Bill Neat that earned him the tag, 'Bravest of the Brave'. Born at Bledlow in Buckinghamshire in 1789, he was known as 'The Battersea Gardener' because that part of London was his place of employment. As well as boxing, he was reputed to be skilled in walking, running and trotting races and to be prominent in the organisation of.'scientific dog fights' and bull-baiting.

Donnelly and Oliver toed the line at 2 p.m., much later than scheduled because of the hitch in fixing the site. Both

Under Broughton's Rules of the Ring, seconds were allowed to stay in the ring with their boxers during fights. As depicted here during the contest between Jack Randall and Jack Martin at Crawley Downs, Sussex, in 1819, the attendants were (from left) Tom Jones and Tom Oliver, for Randall, and Ben Burns and Harry Harmer, for Martin.

One second was known as 'the knee man', his knee being used to support his boxer between rounds (nobody thought of bringing a stool) while the other second was known as 'the bottle man'. He supplied interval refreshments to his man.

men looked calm and confident.

No blows were struck for the first minute or more as the combatants sized each other up warily. The Irish champion attempted the first punch, a left that fell short of its target. Again he tried and again he was out of range.

Angered at his futile efforts, Donnelly moved determinedly into the attack and drove the Englishman back against the ropes. They grappled as each tried desperately to throw his opponent to the ground. After much exertion, both men fell down, with Donnelly on top. The round had lasted five minutes.

Oliver tried his first real punch in the second round, but Donnelly cleverly blocked it with his forearm. There was another tussle by the ropes before they fell, the Irishman again uppermost.

When he returned to 'scratch' for the next round, Oliver was bleeding from the nose and was already showing signs of distress. It was first blood then to Donnelly. The Englishman attacked bravely and forced his rival to retreat to the ropes, where both men tumbled. Cries of 'Well done, Oliver'.

The Englishman followed up his slight advantage at the start of the fourth, but Donnelly neatly blocked most of his attempted body digs. Oliver did connect with one heavy right to the ribs, only to take a fierce left to the face in reply. He staggered back against the ring strands. At close range Donnelly was 'tied up' so he used his head to butt Oliver in the face, an unsporting tactic that drew loud protests from the Englishman's followers. Dan employed his great strength to throw his man with considerable force and Oliver looked badly shaken.

It was Donnelly's turn to shed blood in the fifth round after taking a heavy smash to the mouth, preceded by a solid dig to the stomach that brought down his guard. Once again, however, Dan's strength told at close range when he tossed his rival with a cross buttock.

Cautious sparring marked the start of round six. Light blows were exchanged for about five minutes until Donnelly dropped 'The Battersea Gardener' with a solid right under the heart. Unable to check his attack in time, Dan seemed to land another punch while his opponent was on the ground. The Englishman's cornermen yelled 'Foul' but, after consultation between the umpires, it was ruled an accident.

The blood flowed freely in the seventh round — Oliver from the nose and Donnelly from the mouth — following some heavy exchanges. Oliver landed a good assortment to the body and nipped smartly away from Dan's attempted counters. The Irish champion was floored to end the round, the best to date from Oliver, who grinned broadly as he rested on his second's knee.

Donnelly appeared quite unruffled after the thirty-seconds break. He slipped to the turf and Oliver nearly fell over him. The Englishman's attendants alleged that Donnelly 'lifted his leg with intent to kick Oliver or divert him from his purpose'. The claim was hotly disputed by the Irish corner. The fight was allowed to continue and the contestants wrestled and fell together. Oliver was bleeding profusely.

In the ninth, Donnelly pulled away from a clinch and hit out strongly, mainly with the left hand. He employed a rare right to dig solidly into Oliver's ribs and floor him. So heavily delivered was the punch that Oliver carried the impressions of Dan's knuckles for the remainder of the fight.

Both boxers and their seconds were ever on the alert for any opportunity to gain an advantage, fairly or otherwise. When Oliver was knocked down in the tenth round, his cornerman, Shelton, stuck out his knee to cushion the fall. Tom Belcher, Donnelly's attendant, was so incensed that he yelled across to Shelton a warning that he dare not repeat such action. Shelton insisted that his knee just happened to be in that position when Oliver fell.

It was a topic among the crowd that Donnelly had made little use of his famed right hand, of which the Irish had bragged so much. Was the sledgehammer right' just a myth, like so many of the stories that emanated from the Emerald Isle?

The eleventh and twelfth rounds were quietly contested, with Donnelly each time finishing uppermost in the falls. Twenty-four minutes had now elapsed and it was the Englishman who looked the more tired.

Right from 'scratch' in the 13th, the Irish champion hit
Oliver flush in the mouth and stunned him. Gallantly, Oliver
rallied and the pair wrestled in the middle of the ring trying
to gain a throw. Donnelly pulled himself clear and landed a
hard blow to the throat that left the Englishman hanging
helplessly across the rope. But Dan sportingly stood back
and lifted his arms, refusing to take advantage. Oliver, too
exhausted to be grateful, slumped slowly to the turf.

The English fans had not been given much to cheer about
up to now, but they had a brief moment of elation in the
14th round when their man staggered Donnelly with 'a hard
facer'. Their enthusiasm was soon stifled when Dan stormed
back to beat Oliver to the ground.

In the 15th session Oliver reeled before the Irishman's
attack and went down beside the ropes. Both men showed
the effects of their gruelling ordeal in the next round when
they fell together and their respective seconds had to separate
their entangled bodies.

After some heavy 17th round exchanges, Donnelly
mounted a firm offensive and Oliver was forced to retreat to
all four corners of the ring. Looking very disheartened and
bleeding badly, he slumped to the ground. Donnelly fell on
top of him and his knee caught Oliver in the stomach. Cries
of 'foul' from the English corner were dismissed by the
umpires.

Both men dropped together to end an uneventful 18th
round. A game fight back by Oliver in the next ended when
he fell flat on his face and Donnelly almost finished up on
top of him.

Round 20: one of Dan's rare rights caught his rival on the
eye but there was little force behind it and Oliver just
grinned. Donnelly connected with two good lefts to the head
before they again wrestled each other to the turf, this time
with the Irishman underneath. 'Well done, Oliver', was the
chant from the English fans.

The next three rounds were scrappy. There were few clean
exchanges and each period ended with both men falling
together as they wrestled.

The spectators, who had not been treated to their

expected satisfaction in an uninspiring contest, were somewhat cheered in the 24th round. Oliver nipped in smartly, landed a hard punch to the face and cleverly avoided Donnelly's attempted counters. A fierce exchange ended with the Irish champion dropping to his knees.

'Now, Tom,' said the nobleman who was Oliver's patron, 'go to work, my boy, and you cannot lose it'.

Donnelly appeared for 'scratch' with his face much bloodied. His seconds had been unable to stem the flow from his injured mouth. Oliver scored to the body and skipped away from Dan's wild attempts to hit back. Both landed to the head, but it was the Irishman who went down. Thunderous applause from the English fans. Cribb, Oliver's cornerman, shouted: 'I'll bet a guinea to half a crown on my man'. The current odds were two to one on Oliver.

There was obvious dismay in the Irish corner and little to cheer those who had made the trip from Ireland. 'The Battersea Gardener' was well on top now and looked a certain winner. He cleverly evaded the ponderous attempts of an increasingly more frustrated Donnelly and landed with stiff punches of his own. His constant grinning annoyed the Irish champion even more and Dan showed signs of losing his temper, a fatal error for any boxer. He recklessly charged at Oliver, only to run into a couple of solid smashes that dropped him to the ground.

Donnelly appeared very weak when the two men toed the line for Round 27. Inquirers were told by his seconds that his distressed condition was due to his drinking too much water during the intervals. But, in truth, Dan was paying the penalty of his inadequate preparation and his unrestrained way of life. The round ended when both men tumbled, with Donnelly on top. The Irish fans remained silent as they watched their idol being beaten to the ground in the 28th session.

Donnelly gallantly rallied in the next round but, when they broke from a clinch, the Englishman landed a heavy punch to Dan's much-bloodied mouth. Dan hit back with a good left of his own that staggered Oliver and 'almost put him in want of a dentist'. according to *Boxiana*. Oliver got the better of things in the throw and landed uppermost.

One hour had elapsed when the pugilists squared up for Round 30. Donnelly, who had won the admiration of the English fans for his gameness, countered a body blow with a sharp left to Oliver's face. It momentarily took the grin off the Englishman. They swapped punches evenly until they went down in a tangle, again with Oliver on top.

The 31st round saw Donnelly summoning new reserves of energy and brought joy to his Irish fans. He floored his man with a tremendous left swing and put so much body-weight behind the blow that the momentum almost brought himself down. 'Dan's wind now seemed improved', noted *Boxiana,* 'and the glint of fire had returned to his eye'.

Dan, his confidence growing with his new-found strength, sent Oliver reeling with a smash to the mouth in the 32nd round. The Englishman, however, was living up to his reputation as 'Bravest of the Brave' and seemed prepared to take everything his rival threw at him. 'You might as well be hitting a tree trunk, Donnelly', shouted Shelton from Oliver's corner.

There were several fiery exchanges before Oliver, in turning to avoid a heavy swing, slipped to the ground. Donnelly, unable to check his attack, fell over him.

'Haven't you a right hand, Dan?' inquired Tom Belcher when the Irishman rested on his knee during the interval. 'You must use it now if we are to win'.

Donnelly, at last heeding the advice, crashed a heavy right hand to his opponent's face shortly after the start of round 33. 'Again' yelled Jack Randall. Dan obliged. 'That's the way, my boy', offered Belcher.

Dan again hammered a right to the face, without a reply from his now feeble rival. Oliver grabbed Donnelly as he sank to the ground, bringing Dan with him.

It was almost all over. The 34th round proved to be the last, mercifully for the Englishman. He gamely stuck a left into Donnelly's stomach, then pinned Dan's arms as they clinched. Donnelly, unable to free himself, butted Oliver in the face. As the latter staggered back, Donnelly landed a tremendous right to the ear and then threw Oliver with a mighty cross-buttock.

Oliver was picked up by his seconds. His head hung limply on one shoulder 'as if it had been disconnected'. Frantic efforts were made to revive him in the half-minute rest period, but in vain. He could fight no more. He was still unconscious when 'Time' was called for the next round. The fight had lasted one hour and ten minutes.

Donnelly, declared the winner to ecstatic cheers from his supporters, strode arm-in-arm with his seconds to a nearby farmhouse to rest, while a doctor was summoned to attend to his beaten rival in an adjoining room. Dan expressed unease over Oliver's condition and was relieved to hear that he had recovered his senses.

Before going to the loser's room, Dan thoughtfully concealed Oliver's blue silk handkerchief beneath his own green one. Though it was customary to flaunt a defeated man's coloured silk, the Irish champion had no wish to add to his opponent's distress. For all his faults, he was a warm, sensitive person who always spared a thought for the less fortunate.

Oliver, now recovered, took Donnelly's outstretched hand and the two boxers who, for over an hour had beaten each other with all the strength they could muster, adjourned to a local tavern where they drank each other's health.

Dan then excused himself and went back to the ringside to witness a supporting fight between Lashbrook and Dowd. He had a bet lodged on the result. Later, a barouche and four took him back to the training camp at Riddlesdown, where he spent the night.

The inevitable celebrations began in London the following morning. Boxers, backers and members of the Fancy spent the day drinking, dancing and making merry at Dignam's tavern, the Red Lion in Clare Market. Dan was delighted to welcome Oliver to the party and the two men soon put all thoughts of their grim battle firmly behind them.

The song, *Donnelly's Sprig of Shilelah*, composed by an anonymous fellow-countryman of Donnelly's, was sung at the victory party. The ballad was greeted with loud and prolonged applause.

I

Crawley Common's the place, and who chanced to be there,
Saw an Irishman all in his glory appear,
With his sprig of shilelah and shamrock so green.
When in sweet Dublin city he first saw the light,
The midwife he kick'd, put the nurse in a fright,
But said they, upon viewing him belly and back,
'He's the boy that will serve them all out with a whack,
From his sprig of shilelah and shamrock so green'.

II

He thought about fighting before he could talk,
And instead of a go-cart, he first learn'd to walk,
With his sprig of shilelah and shamrock so green,
George's Quay was his school,
    the right place for good breeding,
Where the boys mind their stops,
    if they don't mind their reading;
There Dan often studied from morning till dark,
And could write, but for shortness, like making his mark,
With his sprig of shilelah and shamrock so green.

III

At his trade, as a chip, he was choice in his stuff,
None pleased him but what was hard, knotty and tough,
Like his sprig of shilelah and shamrock so green.
Nor to strip for his work would he ever refuse,
And right hand and left he the mallet could use,
Length and distance could measure without line or rule,
And at flooring was famous without any tool
But his sprig of shilelah and shamrock so green.

IV

Whenever he arrogance happen'd to meet,
No matter in whom, he took out the conceit,
With his sprig of shilelah and shamrock so green.
To the best of all nations that cross'd Dublin bar,
Dan was ready at tipping a mill or a spar,
The hot-headed Welshmen served out by the lot
And cut up their leeks small enough for the pot,
With his sprig of shilelah and shamrock so green.

V

Hall and Cooper went over with wonderful haste,
On the soil where it grew, they were longing to taste
Of the sprig of shilelah and shamrock so green.
On the plains of Kildare 'twas proposed they should meet
And Donnelly wished to give both a good treat;
Yet to such things as Hall, gallant Dan never stoop'd,
But he took the stout Cooper, and Cooper well hoop'd,
With his sprig of shilelah and shamrock so green.

VI

And as Irishmen always politeness are taught,
He the visit return'd, and to England he brought
His neat sprig of shilelah and shamrock so green.
With the good-natured stranger the English seem'd shy,
And Cooper no more fickle fortune would try;
But at last the game Oliver entered the field
And, tho' on his own soil, was soon forced to yield
To the sprig of shilelah and shamrock so green.

VII

With his kind English friends, he'll again just to please 'em
Soon meet, and if troubled with money, soon lose 'em,
With his sprig of shilelah and shamrock so green.
But if John Bull is wise, he'll from market hang back
And keep all the corn he has got in his sack,
As to him the next season no harvest will bring,
For, like hail, Dan will beat down the blossoms of Spring,
With his sprig of shilelah and shamrock **so green.**

Right – Dan Donnelly at the height of his fame. This portrait, by George Sharples, drawn after a dinner given in the Irish champion's honour at Riddlesdown, Surrey, while he was in training for the fight against Tom Oliver in July, 1819, was pronounced 'life itself' by those present. Dan himself expressed delight at the facsimile of 'me own mug'.

Left – Tom Oliver, who bravely stood up to Donnelly for 34 rounds before being beaten at Crawley Downs, Sussex, in July 1819. Known as 'The Battersea Gardener', though he came from Bledlow, in Buckinghamshire, Oliver beat George Cooper in 17 minutes, but lost to Jack Carter in 46 minutes.

A moderate fighter, his courage was his prime asset. After his retirement, he ran 'The Duke's Head' in Peter Street, Westminster, for a spell.

ONNELLY'S STANDING as a prizefighter was now a great topic among the Fancy. The Irish were more convinced than ever that he could beat any man in the world. The English, having now seen for themselves how he shaped in a serious contest, were less rapturous. Indeed, they were generally of the opinion that he had been much over-rated by the fanciful Irish.

'The Irish champion has not turned out as good a fighter as was anticipated', wrote Pierce Egan in *Boxiana*. 'He is not the decisive, tremendous hitter with the right as calculated. Had he used it earlier, it would probably have ended in half an hour. He is not lacking in gameness and coolness and is a dangerous man in a fall. Donnelly admitted it was a bad fight, that he acted like a wooden man and could not account for it. He frequently hit with an open right hand. He showed little sign of the punishment taken, except that his right ear was slightly marked and his body was reddened and bruised'.

There was much speculation about why he failed to make better use of his much-vaunted right hand. Some said he used it sparingly in order to boost the odds on Oliver and then, when the price was right, he brought the right into play to finish the job. Others believed he hurt the hand in an early round and did not employ it until he knew his man was ready to be knocked out.

The Irish champion himself offered no alibis. He was plainly disappointed with his performance, especially as he had desperately wanted to impress the sceptical English. He stubbornly refused to accept that his reckless mode of living had anything to do with his below-par showing.

Pierce Egan was in no doubt that it was Donnelly's escapades as a 'petticoat poacher' that largely accounted for his 'distressed and blown state' during the Oliver fight.

It took a doctor's examination to at last bring home to the devil-may-care Dubliner the folly of his ways. He was told that he had venereal disease. Or, as Egan, in his picturesque way, explained it: 'It is a well known fact that, after his battle with Oliver, it was not only discovered, but Donnelly acknowledged, that he had unfortunately contracted a disease in the promiscuousness of his amours'.

Donnelly's fall into London's wicked ways was partly blamed on his innocence by W. Buchanan-Taylor in his book *What Do You Know About Boxing?*, he commented: 'London night life and the 'hells' of St. James's put a quick end to the Irish champion's career. He stepped on the toboggan of good living and bad company. The 'hells' referred to were a series of night clubs of the period; worse, indeed, than the most evil of the night haunts of recent years. One of the things missing was the knowledge of hygiene. The total ignorance of Donnelly aided the acquisition of a disability that sent him low. Yet he was still a hero — possibly a victim of ignorance and, far worse, an amateur in regard to pseudo-love. Donnelly could not 'take it' as we now know the phrase'.

Such scandalous news travelled fast — even in the early 19th century. Back in Dublin, Dan's wife took the disclosure calmly and rationally. A paragon of understanding, she blamed her husband's condition on the temptations of London. She had opposed the idea of his going to England in the first place, but accepted that it was the only way to pay off his heavy debts. Whilst it might seem wrong that Mrs. Donnelly did not take a firmer line with her wayward spouse, it has to be acknowledged that Dan rarely yielded to any form of discipline, no matter who tried to impose it in his own interests.

Mrs. Donnelly was sufficiently concerned, nonetheless, as to take the boat to England and seek a heart-to-heart talk with her husband.

Dan was enjoying the company of members of the Fancy at Tom Belcher's place, the Castle Tavern in Holborn, when a porter informed him that Mrs. Donnelly had arrived in London and had taken a room at the White Horse in Fetter Lane, off Fleet Street.

The Irish champion was in a merry mood and he kidded the messenger: 'What sort of a woman is it who wants to see me? Is she a big woman, a good-looking woman?'

'But, sir' exclaimed the startled porter, 'don't you know

your own wife?'

Grinning hugely, Donnelly stood up. 'Never mind,' he said, 'I'll come and have a look at her and see if I know her'.

His wife was asleep in her room when Dan arrived at the inn. She was startled when the curtains around her bed were drawn back and she saw Dan standing there.

'Oh, Dan, is that you?' she said. 'You look so pale I hardly recognise you'.

He chided her. 'Did you think I was dead, then? Have you brought over my coffin?'

After a fiery argument, Mrs. Donnelly could see it was useless trying to get her man to change his ways. But she did get one guarantee — that he would let her stay with him as long as he remained in England.

The loyalty and devotion shown by Dan's wife, especially when he was taking frequent detours off the 'straight and narrow' going on drinking binges and playing around with other women, is indeed quite remarkable. And Dan himself, who seemed unable — or unwilling — to resist the slightest temptation, would always turn to his wife in his moments of remorse and torment.

Nowhere in the publications of the period is Mrs. Donnelly's Christian name mentioned, or how many children the couple had. Only *Blackwood's Magazine,* in its issue of May 1820, referred to 'his beloved Rebecca' and 'his sons'. The editor of *Blackwood's,* Professor John Wilson, who wrote under the name of 'Christopher North', also commented: 'The domestic life of Sir Daniel was marked by all the most endearing features that characterise the tender husband, the fond father, the sincere, the generous friend. Early in life he formed a connection with an amiable and enlightened female of the Society of Friends (Quakers) who was the balm of every wound in life, the soft and pleasing pillow upon which he reclined his head in the awful hour of death'.

But Professor Wilson's writings were not always reliable and the aforementioned 'facts' cannot therefore be regarded as 'gospel'.

Meanwhile, challenges poured in from boxers who, once

fearful of his reputation, were encouraged by his failure to shine in the bout with Oliver and the reports of his poor physical condition.

On August 15, 1819, the following notice appeared in the London *Weekly Dispatch:* 'A challenge to Dan Donnelly, the conqueror of Oliver. I, the undersigned, do hereby offer to fight you for 1,000 guineas at any place and at any time which may be agreeable to you, provided it be in England. Signed: Enos Cope, innkeeper, Macclesfield'.

A nobleman offered Donnelly his choice of opponent from Cooper, Shelton, Gregson, Sutton, Spring, Carter, Neate, Richmond and Painter for a contest at £100-a-side.

Donnelly refused all the invitations to fight. His followers did not know it, nor perhaps did he himself, but he was never again to appear in the ring except to box exhibitions. He was reluctant to even talk about boxing. Especially when in noble company, he would try to steer the conversation away from pugilism, though not always successfully.

His growing aversion to being looked upon as a prize-fighter was typified one night as he dined at one of his favourite spots, the Red Lion in Clare Market. Word reached him that some of his fellow countrymen were gathered downstairs in the Long Room and wished to meet him and shake his hand.

Dan, angered at the intrusion, bellowed: 'Sure what do they take me for – a beast that is to be made a show of? I am no fighting man and I will not exhibit myself to please anybody'.

His companions, at length, managed to persuade him that it would be impolite not to accede to such a simple request. So he went downstairs and entered the Long Room to loud cheers from his delighted fans.

London life was great as long as the cash was there to sustain it. But Dan's financial status was rapidly deteriorating, due to his ring inactivity and his many extravagances.

A trip to 'Hell', as the London West End's more notorious gambling houses were aptly termed, proved a most ill-advised venture as a means towards recouping sorely needed funds.

He lost heavily.

It was 'a great secret, only whispered all over London' that Dan lost £80 in one disastrous night's gambling. He was a great favourite with the Fancy, both English and Irish, and every day and night he was to be found in one tavern or another.

Mrs. Donnelly did not share her husband's enthusiasm for the English capital and, prompted by her wishes, he reluctantly decided to return to Ireland. The annual Donnybrook Fair on the outskirts of Dublin was due to commence shortly and he hit on the idea of setting up a boxing booth there. Two English boxers, his former foe and now his friend, George Cooper, and Bob Gregson agreed to accompany him and spar with him at the fair.

Dan had £20 in his pocket as he waited for the stagecoach to take him to Liverpool, where he would take the steamer to Dublin. That was all he had to show for over six months spent in England. And even that was not to remain his.

Just as he was about to step on board the coach, a bailiff handed him a writ ordering him to pay £18 to his old friend and sparmate, Jack Carter.

'By the powers,' exclaimed the shocked Irishman, 'it is the other way around. Carter is indebted to me'.

Donnelly told the lawman his side of the story. The last time he had met Carter was on May 27, the second day of Epsom Races, when the drunken English pugilist had paraded around the racecourse shouting that he would beat Donnelly either in Ireland or in England.

Dan said he had, in fact, accepted the challenge and put down a £2 deposit for a fight to be arranged with Carter within a month for £500-a-side, or there and then if he so wished.

Neither Carter nor the £2 had he seen since. He vehemently denied that Carter had later deposited £18 and that he (Donnelly) had refused to honour the agreement to fight. It was he who should be suing Carter, he insisted.

The bailiff sympathised with Donnelly, but said he could not withdraw the writ. Dan saw he had no option but to pay up the £18. If he decided to stay on in London to contest the issue, he would not alone forfeit the fare already paid for his wife and himself for the trip to Ireland but would also miss the chance to appear at Donnybrook Fair.

In a great rage, he discharged the writ and ordered the coach-driver to proceed at the gallop. All that remained as the proceeds of his entire English venture was a measly £2.

TRULY THE MOST fanciful of all the legends that surround the name of Dan Donnelly is that he received a knighthood from the Prince Regent (later King George IV). It is said that, on being introduced to the boxer at a banquet in 1819, the Prince remarked: 'I am glad to meet the best fighting man in Ireland'.

To which the brash Donnelly allegedly replied: 'I am not that, your Royal Highness, but I am the best in England'.

The Prince laughed heartily and took so immediate a liking to Dan, we are told, that he bestowed upon him the honour of a knighthood.

> *Our worthy Regent was so delighted*
>
> *with the great valour he did evince*
>
> *that Dan was cited, aye, and invited*
>
> *to 'Come be knighted' by his own Prince.*

Had I been successful in my efforts to find documented proof of the laying of the sword, I would be most happy to record it here. Regrettably, there is no official confirmation of the story.

There is no doubt that Donnelly himself, either for egotistical reasons or as a practical joke, claimed to be 'Sir Daniel'. And his legion of Irish followers readily accepted his word.

Most of the poems and other written tributes published after his death referred to him as 'Sir Daniel', but it is noticeable that neither the inscription on his tombstone in Kilmainham or that on the monument in Donnelly's Hollow on the Curragh paid him any such honour.

Among the pugilistic historians of the period, only Pierce Egan, the editor of *Boxiana*, seems to have lent any support to the legend. But even Egan, who professed to being 'a great advocate of data', admitted he did not witness the sword being laid.

As he 'did not doubt the honour or courage of the fighting hero,' Egan stated that he 'took it for granted that Donnelly

received the knighthood — and that it was an honorary thing altogether, without any tip being demanded'.

Even the venue of the supposed ceremony varies considerably in the written accounts. Nat Fleischer's *Ring Record Book and Boxing Encyclopedia* suggests that the honour was conferred at a banquet given by the Lord Lieutenant of Ireland to Donnelly. But the Prince Regent did not visit Ireland until August 1821, the month after his coronation as King — and eighteen months after Donnelly's death.

It is possible, of course, that the Lord Lieutenant performed the knighthood ceremony in the absence of the Prince and at his command. But this too must be considered improbable.

The date of the monarch's Irish visit would also serve to ridicule the story that he visited Dan at one of his Dublin taverns and 'was so impressed by the Irish champion's physique and unbeaten record that he knighted him on the spot'.

If Prince and pugilist ever did meet, it must be assumed it was in England. Some reports state that the Prince was present at the fight between Donnelly and Oliver at Crawley Downs, Sussex, in July 1819 and that the conferring of the knighthood took place at the winner's celebration party. The Prince was said to have lost a considerable sum of money through betting on Oliver.

This, too, can be discounted. The Prince had not attended a prizefight since he witnessed the brutal battle between his chairman, or sedan carrier, Tom Tyne, and a boxer named Earl at Brighton in 1788. Earl died as a result of the beating he took and, due to the resultant outcry, the Prince publicly announced his disassociation from the sport, though secretly he maintained his interest.

That Donnelly and the Prince met socially is not beyond the bounds of possibility. The Irish boxer was frequently invited to banquets and gatherings of the nobility, where his charm and ready wit made him a popular guest.

Among his admirers was said to be Lord Byron. A staunch supporter of boxing, Byron, though handicapped by a foot deformity since birth, had been an earnest pupil of

Left — The Prince of Wales at the age of 45. He became Regent of the United Kingdom of Great Britain and Ireland three years later, in 1811, on his father, George III, being declared insane. As George IV, he reigned for ten years until his death from a burst blood vessel.

'Gentleman' John Jackson, the former champion of England. He often sparred with Jackson, whom he termed 'the Professor of Pugilism', at the instructor's rooms at 13 Bond Street, London.

But Byron and Donnelly never met. The famed poet and romantic fled England for good in 1816, three years before the boxer set foot on English soil for the first and only time. Nor did Donnelly ever venture further afield than England. If Byron did follow the Irishman's adventures, then he did so from afar. In 1819, while Donnelly was occasionally taking life seriously in England, Byron was living in Ravenna with his mistress, Countess Guiccioli, and beginning to interest himself in Italian revolutionary politics. He contracted a fever and died in Greece in 1824.

An amusing story, which cannot be verified, is told of the day Donnelly met the Duke of Clarence (later King William IV) at the Castle Tavern, in Holborn, London. The pub was held at the time by Tom Spring, and the English pugilist promised to introduce Dan to the Duke. Concerned that 'the uncouth son of Erin' might commit some breach of etiquette, Spring decided to give him some tips on matters of conduct. 'When you address the Duke, always begin by saying 'Your Grace,' he advised Dan.

A day or two later, Donnelly was introduced to the Duke. Making a low and awkward bow, he blurted out: 'For what I am about to receive, O Lord, make me truly thankful'. To which the smiling Duke replied 'Amen' and slipped a guinea into the Irishman's hand.

Later, Spring remonstrated with Donnelly for asking the Duke for money. To which Dan pleaded: 'But sure I didn't ask him for a penny. You told me to say 'Your Grace' and that's all I did'. And the two boxers enjoyed a hearty laugh over the incident.

The Prince Regent's admiration for boxers stemmed from the cult of manliness which was manifest during that period. He looked upon pugilists as the true conception of manliness. He had an avowed dislike of homosexuals and this practice was one of the few vices not to be found among the Prince's circle.

Not that his association with such people as prizefighters helped win the Royal personage any great acclaim. His heavy drinking, loose morals and wild extravagances at a time of economic hardship had already assured him of widespread unpopularity.

For his coronation in July 1821, George IV (as he was now) caused renewed controversy over his association with boxers by engaging eighteen of England's leading pugilists to act as bodyguards. Their role was to guard the King from possible attackers during the procession through the streets and later, if necessary, to act as 'chuckers out' of unauthorised intruders at the ceremony.

Among the prizefighters honoured for the occasion were Donnelly's last opponent Tom Oliver, as well as the Irish champion's former sparmates and associates Jack Carter, Tom Spring, Tom Belcher, Bill Richmond, Ben Burns and Harry Harmer. The English champion Tom Cribb also took part.

The hiring of the boxers by the King was condemned as the act of a frightened bully, but the monarch was so pleased with the way they performed their duties that he ordered the Lord Chamberlain to send a letter of thanks to each man. He also had a golden coronation medal cast which was later raffled and won by Tom Belcher.

But for all his fondness for those of the fistic breed, none but Dan Donnelly, we are expected to believe, so impressed George IV as to be awarded a knighthood. Is it feasible that Donnelly, an Irishman, should have been the chosen one above renowned English prizefighters like Cribb or Spring?

In support of the legend, it is certainly true that George IV had a warm affection for the Irish people, as did they for him. He always felt at ease in the company of Irishmen and professed to a sympathetic understanding of most of their country's problems. Consequently, he was more popular with most of the Irish people than ever he was at home.

A measure of his depth of feeling for his Irish subjects was the fact that he chose Ireland as the first place to visit after his coronation. No reigning English sovereign had ever set foot on Irish soil since the time of Richard II. He charmed the people with his friendliness and approachability, with the easy, natural way he shook them by the hand, talked to them and smiled at them. One elderly Dubliner, voicing a common sentiment, remarked: 'I was a rebel to old King George (the 3rd) in '98, but by God I'd die a hundred deaths for his son, because he's a real king and asks us how we are'.

Perhaps the nearest to an explanation of the legend of 'Sir Daniel' is given by Pierce Egan, the London-bred son of an Irish emigrant pavier, whose quaint style of writing somewhat obscures his value as probably the greatest chronicler of boxing.

In *Boxiana,* Egan referred to 'Sir Daniel' as a 'Knight of the Most Ancient Order of the Fives'. He said: 'This Order takes the precedence of all others. It is an act of nature and was acknowledged in estimation before the existence and authority of kings and emperors. The use of the 'fives' originated with Ould Adam, and Eve also had a 'finger' in it, and it was handed down from generation to generation. It also proved of most essential service to St. Patrick in carrying his cross to Ireland.

'In the revival of the Order of the Fives then, in the person of the champion of Ireland, by his royal highness the Prince Regent, the warm-hearted and generous people of Ireland applauded this heroic act to the skies'.

If any sense is to be made of Egan's account, it would seem to suggest that Donnelly was honoured for his ability with his hands, the mythical 'Order of the Fives' being restricted to those who used their hands to advantage. Even today, the closed fist is often referred to as a 'bunch of fives'.

Were it true that Donnelly was made a 'Sir,' it would be the first and only occasion that a boxer, either in the days of bare-knuckle battling or modern gloved combat, was so honoured by a member of the British Royal Family. He was also said to be the last person knighted during the Regency.

The legend of the Prince Regent's elevation of Ireland's ring hero to the rank of 'Sir' is fully in keeping with the period, one of the most romantic, extravagant and wildly contrasting in English history. It produced more than its share of extraordinary characters, none more complex than

The public entry of King George IV to Dublin on the gloriously sunny day of August 17, 1821. This was the scene of enormous welcome he received at what is now the site of the Parnell Monument.

Wearing the Order of St. Patrick on his Field Marshall's uniform, the King stood up in his open carriage waving his hat, pointing to the huge bunch of shamrock attached to it, and then laying his hand on his heart, acknowledging the cheers of the dense throng.

Perhaps the commonly believed story of the 'knighthood' he bestowed on their late boxing champion while Prince Regent helped win him the admiration of the Irish, a feeling he reciprocated.

the Regent himself. An overweight, vain 'spoilt child,' he wasted enormous sums of money on satisfying his frequent whims to change the entire structure and decor of his many places of residence. He even altered his birthday because the date didn't suit him!

'The Regency was comparatively brief but had a character, a tone, a tang, all its own,' wrote J. B. Priestly in his book *The Prince of Pleasure and his Regency 1811-20.*

Priestly brilliantly summarised the great contrasts of attitudes, of behaviour, of conditions, and the larger than life personalities of the period. 'Down one side of the street may be seen the evangelicals, the prigs and the prudes, and down the other go the gamesters, the extravagant dandies, the drunken womanisers... the age swings between extremes of elegance and refinement and depths of sodden brutality and misery. It has no common belief, no accepted code, no general standard of conformity. It seems horrible one moment, enchanting the next.

'Anything and everything can be happening. In the North (of England), some men are inventing and setting up new machines while other men are going by night with huge hammers to break them. Wellington is having fifty men flogged while Wordsworth is gazing at a celandine. Jane Austen is sending Mansfield Park to her publishers; Lady Caroline Lamb is sending Lord Byron clippings of pubic hair. Wilberforce is denouncing the slave trade while Beau Brummell is denouncing with equal gravity an imperfectly-tied cravat.

'In a city (London) where many people think it is wicked to row a boat on Sunday, young noblemen lose £25,000 in a night at Waiter's, tiny boys of six are forced up chimneys, prostitutes of fourteen roam the streets. Down at Brighton, in his fantastic Pavilion, the Regent is believed to be staging wild orgies, perhaps with kidnapped virgins, when in fact, with his stays loosened over the curacao, he is giving imitations of cabinet ministers to amuse the grandmothers who are his favourites. All appearances tend to be deceptive; too many public personages are either drunk or a trifle cracked...'

One anonymous poet had no doubt as to where Donnelly ranked among the great men of battle when he penned these lines.

Ye may prate of your Wellingtons, Bluchers and Neys,

And smother them over with blarney and praise,

But greater than all was that Knight of the fist,

Who bate all the boxers he met on the list,

Sir Dan Donnelly.

Lord Byron (in dressing gown) sparring with 'Gentleman' John Jackson at the former English champion's boxing academy in Bond Street, London. Though handicapped by a club-foot, the famed poet learned the rudimentary skills of the sport from the acknowledged 'Professor of Pugilism'. Jackson closed his academy in 1824, the year of Byron's death. Such was the respect in which Jackson was held by the nobility that when George IV was crowned in 1820, the former champion was chosen to head a bodyguard of famous prizefighters.

WHETHER THEY recognised him as 'Sir Daniel' or not, his fellow country-men gave Donnelly a welcome befitting a king on his return to his native shores. Thousands of excited Irish men, women and children — rich and poor alike — lined the quayside as the packet steamer docked at the Pigeon House after its twenty-three hour journey from Liverpool. Cries of 'Welcome home, Dan' and 'Donnelly for ever' echoed across Dublin Bay.

Dan had expected a hearty reception, but not one of this magnitude. People had waited for hours to greet their hero and minor skirmishes broke out as many sought to touch him. A white horse had been kept in readiness to carry the conquering hero in triumph through the streets of his native Dublin and Donnelly laughed delightedly as a couple of brawny men hoisted him onto the animal's back.

The city streets were lined with crowds cheering the return of the Irish champion. So many people were gathered at Townsend Street, Dan's birthplace, that the procession was forced to a halt. Donnelly expressed his gratitude to the people for their warm reception and, with a final flourish of his famed right fist, he dismounted and retired to a local tavern to drink a toast to their health. As many of his fans as could cram into the bar joined in the festivities which went on into the small hours.

Donnybrook Fair opened on August 27, 1819. The world-famous fair had been staged annually for over six hundred years and, for the two weeks it lasted, it was a scene of wild merrymaking and frequent drunken brawls.

Various sideshows included 'horse tumbling, sleight of hand, serious and comic singing and the music of the bagpipes and fiddle'. But the real fun was at night, when things really started swinging.

As well as providing nightly exhibitions of various enter-tainments, there were inevitable fights in which fists, sticks and bottles were used with gay abandon. Hence the term of a 'Donnybrook' to describe a wild brawl.

Clearly Donnybrook Fair was no place for any self-respecting female to be seen. Taking account of the number of 'painted prostitutes, drunken youths and lassies' found there, the *Dublin Penny Journal* ventured to say that 'there is more misery and madness, devilment and debauchery than could be found crowded into any equal space of ground in any part of this globe. It has been calculated that during the period of Donnybrook Fair there is more loss of female character and greater spoilation of female virtue among the lower orders than during all the other portions of the year'.

Donnybrook Fair, 1830. This print depicts the common unruly scene as stick-wielding antagonists, beggars, drunks, gamblers, prostitutes and public orators vie for the attention of patrons along with the various sideshows, improvised shops and drinking tents.

The world-famous fair caused such an annual outcry that it was finally abolished in 1855. Dan Donnelly's boxing booth was the main attraction in 1819 – but the Irish champion preferred the drinking places, much to the disgust of those who had paid to see him in the ring.

The tents housing the various sideshows were erected on grass and were formed of sticks and sods covered with old sheets, petticoats and rags. Inside most, benches were installed along the sides for customers to witness the exhibitions.

The main attraction at Donnybrook Fair in 1819 was undoubtedly Dan Donnelly's boxing booth. A ten-foot square ring was erected in the tent and, for a moderate admission fee, visitors were invited to see the Irish champion in sparring matches with his two English partners, George Cooper and Bob Gregson.

A song was specially composed for the occasion and was printed on sheets for sale to patrons. Entitled *Donnybrook Fair,* the song was in itself an adequate description of the occasion. Sung to the tune of *Robin Adair,* the words were as follows:

What made the town so dull?
    Donnybrook Fair.
What made the tents so full?
    Donnybrook Fair.
Where was the joyous ground
Booth, tent and merry-go-round?
    Donnybrook Fair.

Beef, mutton, lamb and veal,
    Donnybrook Fair.
Wine, cider, porter, ale,
    Donnybrook Fair.
Whiskey, both choice and pure,
Men and maids most demure,
Dancing on the ground flure
    Donnybrook Fair.

Where was the modest bow?
    Donnybrook Fair.
Where was the friendly row?
    Donnybrook Fair.
Where was the fun and sport,
Where was the gay resort?
Where Sir Dan held his court,
    Donnybrook Fair.

For the first few days of the fair, the crowds flocked to the boxing booth. They were disappointed to find Donnelly refusing to take the sparring sessions seriously. He laughed, joked and clowned through most of his appearances and 'only occasionally demonstrated how things might be done in the ring'.

Much of the blame was laid on Donnelly's adoring followers who, according to a contemporary journal, 'constantly gave him drops of the cratur and thus prevented him from exerting himself'.

Very often Dan, suffering from an outsize hangover, would fail to show up for his scheduled sparring match. As a result, most of the boxing was left to Cooper and Gregson. The scientific skill of Cooper, still remembered with affection by the Irish for his courageous losing battle against Donnelly at the Curragh four years earlier, was especially appreciated by the daily audiences. But it was the Irish champion the people had paid their money to see and they were not slow in voicing their disapproval of his absences.

When word got around that Donnelly's billed appearances could not be guaranteed, attendances at the boxing booth grew smaller. So what had looked like proving a lucrative fortnight for the three boxers did not live up to expectations, thanks to Donnelly's failure to stay sober even for that long.

A further sour note was introduced when Jack Carter turned up at Donnybrook Fair. For several days, in a drunken stupor, he staggered around from tent to tent looking for Donnelly and calling for a fight with the Irish champion. 'The Lancashire Hero,' whose action in having a writ served on Dan had earned him few admirers, even among the English, had followed Donnelly to Ireland with the hope of getting a match with him.

Carter's obnoxious behaviour went largely unnoticed at the fair, where such carry-on was normal. So rowdy did the annual event prove that a lengthy campaign for its abolition was finally successful and the last Donnybrook Fair was held in 1855. Though now a respectable Dublin suburb, the name of Donnybrook is still associated with 'merry making, whiskey drinking and skull cracking'.

Carter continued to pester Donnelly for a fight after the fair ended. In a letter to the *Dublin Journal* of September 18, he claimed that Dan had failed to answer his earlier challenge for a match at £200-a-side.

Two days later, in the same paper, Carter's allegation was refuted in a letter from 'a committee of friends and supporters of Donnelly'. The group claimed that Dan had already accepted the challenge and that they, his friends, had lodged £200 in his support. They said they had made appointments for an interview but 'neither Carter or his friends, if he has any', had attended.

Parties representing both boxers ultimately met at 20 Fownes Street, Dublin, and signed a provisional agreement for a fight between Donnelly and Carter. Mr. W. Dowling deposited £20 as a guarantee on Donnelly's behalf and Mr. L. Byrne did likewise for Carter. The deposits were held by John Dooly. The parties agreed to meet again on October 5 to increase the guarantees to fifty guineas each side.

If either of the parties did not honour the scheduled date of the next meeting, it was decided that the original deposit of £20 would be forfeited. The proposed date of the fight was November 25. It would be at a place within thirty miles of Dublin, the exact venue to be decided by the toss of a coin. The purse money would be £200.

The news of the proposed match brought delight to Donnelly's vast legion of supporters. Not for four years had he a serious prizefight on Irish soil and they were anxious to see what improvements he had gained from his spell in England. Carter, a talented performer in the ring, would provide a good test.

Alas, they were doomed to disappointment. The fight never took place. Donnelly, when the parties representing the boxers met on October 5, insisted that he would only meet Carter on a winner-take-all basis and that the total stake money be deposited with a person of his own choice.

Carter, not surprisingly, refused to fight on these terms. He recalled that Tom Hall and George Cooper had both complained of unfair treatment when they met Donnelly on his native turf and he angrily denounced the Irish champion for not agreeing to a share of the purse.

The meeting broke up with each side hurling abuse and accusations of trickery and cowardice at each other. It was especially sad to see the two former friends and business associates, Donnelly and Carter, ending up such bitter antagonists.

Neither man was blameless for the break-up. Carter's action in suing Donnelly for almost every penny of his English earnings was heartless. And no one could excuse his drunken abuse of the Irish champion during the Donnybrook Fair. Donnelly, on the other hand, was not prepared to test his strength and skill against Carter in a prize fight unless the odds were slanted in his own favour.

In Donnelly's case, his demands to have things his own way, even if it meant employing unfair tactics, was in contrast to his normal generous nature.

This stubborn side was shown on another occasion when one of his proteges, Pat Halton, fought Jack Langan on the Curragh. Halton, known as 'Donnelly's Boy', had been taught the art of boxing by Dan and, for a time, he looked like emulating his tutor as Irish champion. He failed to live up to his early promise, however, and took a severe beating from Langan, one of the best Irish pugilists of the bare-knuckle era.

After an hour of battling, Halton had clearly lost heart and was pounded to the turf by Langan. Donnelly was one of Halton's cornermen and he tried desperately to revive his charge in the half-minute rest period. When he failed to do so, Langan, quite rightly, claimed victory. But Donnelly at last got his battered protege to his feet and insisted that the fight continue.

Langan's seconds maintained that their man was the rightful winner because Halton failed to toe the line in time, but still Donnelly insisted that the fight continue. Langan refused to re-commence the contest and Donnelly would not consent to giving him the purse. Angry words were exchanged and the match ended in uproar.

Later that evening, Langan traced Donnelly to the Cockpit Inn and remonstrated with him for his unsporting behaviour.

Jack Langan, Donnelly's successor as Champion
of Ireland. A great admirer of Donnelly,
Langan was instructed in the art of boxing by Dan. They
later had a row which soured Langan's view of his
hero somewhat. Langan was twice defeated
in savage battles with the English
Champion Tom Spring.

Dan had been his idol and it saddened him to be treated this way.

The row reached a height when Langan shouted bitterly: 'I know, Dan, you could beat me. Yet I will hold you a wager that you do not lick me in half an hour if we fight right now'.

Donnelly turned down the challenge and, after some more argument, he reluctantly agreed to give Langan the purse money.

It was clearly evident by now that the Irish champion had no real desire ever to box again, although his supporters still cherished the hope that he could be persuaded to re-enter the ring. Dan, now more than ever, abhorred the rigours of training, such little as he did, and could not face the thought of preparing for a serious contest. Though outwardly in the prime of health, he was still suffering from the effects of the V.D. he had contracted in London and was drinking more than ever. He did not realise, or chose to ignore, the greater damage he was doing to his much abused body.

As a publican, Donnelly seemed at last to have found the right formula for success. His latest Dublin premises, at the corner of Greek Street and Pill Lane (now Chancery Street), at the back of the Four Courts, reported a brisk trade. The tavern was especially popular with farmers up from the country to do business at the nearby fruit and vegetable market. They took delight in calling at Donnelly's place for the privilege of shaking his hand and drinking his porter.

His fame established and, revelling in the popularity it had earned him, Dan enjoyed nothing better than to chat and joke with his customers 'and drink his glass dry'.

Dan's old friend turned antagonist, Jack Carter, had taken up residence in Dublin and held the licence of 'The Black Lion' at Kilmainham, while Bob Gregson was another boxer-turned-publican in Moore Street. Prizefighting, obviously, was a popular topic of the day in the Irish capital.

Donnelly, banishing forever all thoughts of a ring comeback, looked to new fields to conquer. His strong personality and gift for public speaking gave him the idea that he might try his hand at politics and campaign for justice for his down-trodden fellow Catholics, a cause very close to his heart.

Another Daniel — O'Connell — was then struggling for support for his emancipation campaign, but was still some years from seeing at least part of his dream realised. In the meantime Irish Catholics, though freed from the worst of the Penal Laws, still struggled with injustices such as the payment of tithes to the Established (Protestant) Church and the limiting of the vote to owners of freehold property worth over forty shillings (£2). No Catholic could be a member of Parliament although four-fifths of the Irish nation were of that faith. Nor could one hold any public office even at a local level.

Twice in Donnelly's own lifetime, the frustration of the Irish Catholic population had boiled over into rebellion. But the revolts led by Wolfe Tone in 1798 and by Robert Emmet in 1803 had proved abortive and the mood was now more towards political agitation.

In Dan Donnelly, the suppressed Irish saw not just a champion prizefighter — but a champion of their cause. By his stirring victories over top-ranked English pugilists, he symbolised ultimate success in Ireland's long, bitter fight for freedom from her oppressors.

Donnelly was intensely proud of being Irish and made no apologies for his nationality when the English sought his companionship when he attained fame as a boxer. They could take him as he was or not at all.

Dan had no time for those who brought scorn upon his native land. On one occasion, someone was rash enough to praise Peter Corcoran as possibly a better Irish pugilist than he. Donnelly angrily retorted: 'Bloody end to his soul! He sold out his country and that's something I'll never do'.

Corcoran, the first Irishman to win the heavyweight championship of England, lost the title in 1776 to Harry Sellars in a fight that was widely held to be 'fixed'. Corcoran prospered from the proceeds of the contest, but lost the friendship of his admirers and when he died he had to be buried by subscription.

Donnelly, however, did not pursue his ambition to enter

the political arena, He probably realised, or was wisely counselled, that he would face even tougher fighting and take more severe buffeting than ever he took in the prizering.

Lord Byron was apparently convinced that Donnelly, if not a politician, would have made an excellent bishop. In Venice when he heard of the Irish champion's death in 1820, the poet allegedly remarked: 'Dan would have been a great man in the pulpit'.

ON THE MORNING of February 15, 1820, Dan complained to his wife of feeling dull and heavy. He dismissed it, however, as a trifling cold, probably brought on by a strenuous game of 'fives' the previous day. He had finished the ball game in a great state of perspiration and drank a large quantity of water before cooling off.

Dan spent some time in his Pill Lane public house chatting to customers but, finding it difficult to breathe, he decided to take a walk in the hope that the fresh air would clear his lungs. It was a mistake. He had not gone far when he felt himself weak and trembling. He returned to the tavern.

Not wishing to disclose his illness, he spent some more time with his customers until he finally was forced to excuse himself and went upstairs to lie down in bed.

When Mrs. Donnelly closed the bar at midnight, she was alarmed to find her husband's condition had worsened. Dan spent a very restless night and, the next morning, she sent for a doctor.

She was shocked to be told that the doctor held little hope of Dan's recovery. But she refused to accept that he would succumb to a sudden illness. Wasn't he a man above ordinary mortals? Hadn't he proved his strength and resilience many times in the prizering? And wasn't it also true that, for all his reckless ways, he had never had a serious day's illness in his life?

She comforted herself by recalling how Dan had told her of the time when, as an adventurous youth of twenty, he had gone to the North of Ireland in search of work as a carpenter and some amusement. Tired and hungry after spending his meagre earnings in various country inns, he had failed to hitch a lift back to Dublin and had spent the night sleeping on a tombstone in a graveyard. He awoke none the worse of his exposure to the chilly night air.

And many was the occasion when he had staggered from a bar at closing time in the pouring rain and, too drunk to head home, he would lie down in a coach-house doorway or on the floor of an uninhabited cellar, his body absorbing the dampness of his clothes.

On frequent drinking sprees with friends, he would eat nothing for three or four days, consuming only whiskey or porter. He scorned all well-meant advice to look after his health, stubbornly convinced that his God-given strength would resist any illness. It turned out to be a sadly misguided assumption.

Dan slept soundly on the day of the doctor's visit until 11 p.m., when he awoke in a state of convulsion. Mrs. Donnelly expressed her alarm but was pacified when he seemed to calm down again after a few turbulent hours. At seven o'clock in the morning, Dan was in great pain and was rapidly weakening. His wife asked him if she should send for a priest. He nodded his agreement.

The priest administered the Last Rites and the brave prize-fighter managed a weak smile of gratitude. He felt a sense of relief that he would not have to depart this life and meet his maker without some effort at repentance for his sins.

There was a brief suggestion that the Irish champion would yet postpone death's knockout blow. Again exhibiting the remarkable powers of recovery that had characterised his ring battles, he felt well enough at mid-day as to ask his son to fetch his clothes so he could go downstairs and join his customers. He managed to dress himself and, with his arms across his boy's shoulders, he rose to walk across the bedroom. He only got as far as a couch when he collapsed.

At one o'clock on the Saturday morning of February 18, 1820, Dan, his head cradled in his sobbing wife's arms, finally gave up the fight. Just before he died, he passed judgement upon himself when he said: 'I have been given so much and I have done so little'.

Pierce Egan, in *Boxiana,* described Dan's death thus: 'In the midst of a gay laughing scene, one of the ugliest customers Dan had ever met with introduced himself, without making any previous match or agreeing as to 'Time' and, cruel to relate, gave the Irish champion such a flooring hit that all the wind in his body was knocked out in a twinkling. He never saw the 'scratch' afterwards and poor Dan closed his ogles for ever upon the prize ring'.

The obituary notice in *Carrick's Morning Post* read: 'Died, at his porter house in Greek Street, Mr. Dan Donnelly, known in the pugilistic school as the Champion of Ireland. It is said that he overheated himself a few days back playing rackets and his death was caused by inflammation of the lungs. He was about 40 years of age. His unexpected and rather sudden death will be deeply lamented by the Fancy. The amateurs declare that no other antagonist, save grim Death, could have milled him off the stage. Peace to his manes'.

The Freeman's Journal differed in its account of his age and the cause of his death. He was 'in his 44th year' and his passing was 'in consequence of his bursting a blood vessel'.

Saunder's Newsletter did not mention his age and adopted an equally cautious note on what killed him. The paper commented that there were 'many rumours respecting this individual's sudden death but, as we have not received any authentic information as yet concerning it, we merely announce the circumstance'.

One of the wilder rumours, that Donnelly's drink had been poisoned by a jealous Englishman, was firmly quashed when the post mortem revealed that he had died of 'natural causes'. Like the varying accounts of his age at the time of his death (it is generally accepted that he was a month short of his 32nd birthday), the exact cause of his death is not recorded.

Perhaps he did pay the penalty, as suggested, for his carelessness following the lively ball game. His habit of drinking large amounts of water while perspiring often aroused misgivings among those who watched him in training. In one of the four taverns he ran (probably the one in Pill Lane/Greek Street), he had a makeshift gymnasium in a back room. Customers who watched him working out with heavy dumbells and punching a sawdust-filled sack were often surprised to see him swallow lots of water and then go back to his training. But whether or not this custom could have caused his death is debatable.

Perhaps sclerosis of the liver, so common with heavy drinkers, or the effects of the lingering V.D., then a much more difficult thing to cure than nowadays, could have caused or contributed to his sudden passing. They can only be matters of conjecture.

It could be that the truth of what caused his death was deliberately hushed up in order to spare his family further sorrow and to parry the ready accusations of the English that the Irish champion was too foolhardy in his way of living to ever have posed a serious threat to the ring supremacy of their own Cribb or Spring.

Whatever indiscretions may have been committed by their departed hero, the Irish showed they were more than willing to forgive. Quite astonishing scenes of national mourning followed the announcements of his death. Truly no popular figure in Irish history was more widely grieved by the common people.

On the morning of the funeral, shops and businesses were closed as a mark of respect. Theatres kept their doors shut for the day. In the Phoenix Park, guns were fired in a salute.

As the funeral procession left at 10 a.m. from his last residence in Greek Street, the late champion's gloves rested upon a silk cushion in the hearse. All along the route, crowds lined the streets and many joined the long train of mourners. From all over the country they came, many of them weeping openly as the flower-laden coffin passed through Capel Street, Great Britain Street (now Parnell Street), Sackville Street (now O'Connell Street) and over Carlisle Bridge (later rebuilt and renamed O'Connell Bridge) to Dan's birthplace in Townsend Street.

Donnelly's popularity with the poorer classes was noted by the *Sporting Magazine,* which reported that 'at least 80,000 men, women and children attended the funeral, the roads and streets leading to the burial ground being covered with a moving mass of rags and wretchedness. No tumult or disturbance whatever occurred'.

After passing College Green, the cortege progressed through Dame Street, Castle Street, Skinners' Row (Christchurch Place), High Street and Cornmarket into Thomas Street. At this point the horse was unyoked and several followers of the late champion proudly pulled the hearse the rest of the way to the burial place at the Royal Hospital Fields, or 'Bully's Acre', at Kilmainham.

'Not a sound was heard as the coffin was lowered into the grave save for the lamentations of the family,' noted a contemporary journal.

A legend exists that Donnelly shares the grave of Prince Murrough, who fell with his father, King Brian Boru, at the Battle of Clontarf in 1014. Murrough was said to have been buried at the foot of an ancient stone cross, only the stump of which remains. Around 1800 the cross fell and, when being re-erected, a huge sword, perhaps owned by Murrough, and a hoard of Danish coins were found at the base. The coins are now in the National Museum, Dublin.

The Dublin Penny Journal supported the story that Murrough's grave was shared by another national hero when, after a lapse of eight hundred years, it took the remains of Dan Donnelly.

'The victor of Clontarf and the victor of Kildare; the pride of the aristocracy and the idol of the people — they now sleep in the same grave,' said the newspaper in its issue of August 25, 1832.

There is no proof that Murrough was actually buried in the Bully's Acre — although the fact that the Irish camp was based at Kilmainham before the Battle of Clontarf lends some credence to the legend. It is certainly untrue, however, that Donnelly's remains lie at the site of the great cross. The boxer's grave is, in fact, some distance from there.

Today, only a huge flat stone covers the last resting place of Ireland's most renowned boxing idol. There is no discernible inscription, nothing to indicate to the observer that this is Donnelly's grave. I was only able to trace it through the help of a long-serving groundsman who had himself learned of its location from older people in the area.

This might suggest that Donnelly was quickly forgotten by his adoring followers. Indeed not. A handsome table-shaped tomb enclosed by railings was erected over his grave but the memorial, as *Dalton's History of County Dublin* put it in 1838, 'is now as extinct as the champion himself'.

It had been Dan's dying wish 'that no external pomp shall

mark my grave'. However, his legion of admirers had concluded that it would not be fitting to let his memory grow dim without some permanent reminder of the thrills and sense of nationalistic pride he had brought them.

A fortnight after his death, a committee of twelve was formed at a meeting in Bergin's Great Rooms in Fleet Street, Dublin. Publican Patrick Bergin was appointed treasurer, his duty being to collect the funds raised by public subscription to build a memorial.

All the publicans throughout the city who had known and admired the late champion were requested to put collection boxes on their counters. The public responded so generously that by May 1, the day the fund closed, a total of £2,327 had been raised.

Scores of suggested epitaphs for the inscription to be put on the tomb were considered by the committee. That contributed by Mr. Halliday, 'inventor of the Kent bugle and author of the celebrated pamphlet on Logier's musical system,' was considered the most suitable.

Halliday's fitting tribute was carved on the memorial. It read as follows:

Dan rests beneath, still hold his memory dear,
Around his tomb let fall the pitying tear;
Now mingled with his kindred dust he lies,
In silence sleepeth — never more to rise
Except on that fateful day when all,
Living and dead, shall hear the trumpet's call.

Death, Tyrant Death, that fell relentless foe,
Our champion levell'd, by a mortal blow;
None else, in single combat, could him harm,
No human foe resist his mighty arm.
Erin lament; bear in record his name;
Lament the man who fought to crown your fame,
Laid prostrate Cooper, Oliver and Hall,
Yielding to none, but Death, who conquers all.

The initial letter in each line, read downwards, spelled out the champion's name.

The attractive memorial remained intact for a few years until it was wrecked one night by members of a Scottish regiment supposedly on guard duty at the adjacent Royal Hospital. The shameful deed caused such public indignation that the regiment was removed from Dublin.

In order to safeguard the grave from further desecration, the broken tombstone was removed and, in belated respect to Donnelly's dying wish, a plain unmarked stone was laid in its place.

The fact that Donnelly was buried in the Bully's Acre would suggest that he was penniless, or virtually so, when he died. According to D'Alton's *History of County Dublin,* it was the only free graveyard for the poor of the city. 'People buried there were unable to meet the burial charges at city churches'.

The popular name given to the graveyard has several suggested origins. One account claims it was known as the Bully's Acre because of the number of tough characters buried there. 'Some of those interred there were as alone and friendless in death as in life,' said another scribe of the period. But the name is more likely a derivative of the Bailli's Acre, named after a high officer of the Knights Hospitallers, whose priory is now the Royal Hospital at Kilmainham.

No indication of Donnelly's financial state was given in any publication at the time of his death. Nor could I find any record of a will he might have left.

T. G. Hazard, author of *The Life of Dan Donnelly,* published in 1820, maintained that at the time of Donnelly's death his public house in Pill Lane was doing a brisk trade and 'he was well on the way to making a rapid fortune'. But Hazard's book is over-patronising with regard to his late hero and he was probably too close to Donnelly's family to dwell on such unpleasantries as his true financial status.

It is most unlikely that Donnelly owned any of the four Dublin taverns he ran at different times. It was the custom then for the actual owner to install a popular figure as landlord, or mine host, as the English term it, in the hope of drawing more customers.

Bearing in mind his reckless mode of living, there seems little doubt that Donnelly had no ready 'nest egg' to pass on to his sorrowing widow. The heavy debts he ran up in England and at home would have seen to that.

The remains of an ancient stone cross in the Bully's Acre burial ground at Kilmainham. Legend claims it marks the grave of Prince Murrough, son of Brian Boru, who died in battle at Clontarf in 1014. After a lapse of 800 years, according to some accounts, Murrough's grave was shared with the remains of Dan Donnelly, but this is a fallacy. The boxer's grave is actually some distance from the old cross.

IF DAN DONNELLY, in the few short years of his fame, filled the void in his followers' lives by becoming their champion, their hero, their demigod — then his sudden death assured him of martyrdom. Poets, writers and ballad composers penned their sorrows in a great profusion of published tributes to the departed pugilist. The journals of the day were full of letters of lamentation and poetic lines of homage to his memory.

Throughout the land, the shock of Dan's demise was deeply felt. Typical of the harrowing scenes were those which marked the meeting of the Cork Philosophical and Literary Society on March 22, 1820, just over a month after he took the fatal count.

The guest speaker at the society's meeting was Richard Dowden, who had been a close friend of Donnelly and had been instructed in the art of boxing by him.

A magnificent full-length painting of the late champion, specially executed for the occasion by the society's portrait painter, Mr. Topp, hung on the wall behind the president's chair. The painting was solemnly draped in black ribbon and was lit by six oil lamps.

Tears welled in the eyes of the attentive members as Dowden began his sad address: 'He, who but a few short days ago was the glory of our land; he, whose intellectual and corporal energies were the theme of every tongue; he, who basked in all the sunshine of prosperity; he, who in all the pride of conscious dignity stood on the loftiest pinnacle of fame and honour; he, whose virtues were as the refreshing dews of Heaven; he — is gone!'

Dowden's speech was interrupted by the uncontrollable sobbing of several lady members, who begged to be excused. The menfolk took advantage of the enforced break to blow into their handkerchiefs and gulp their drinks in vain attempts to ease the dryness in their throats.

Dowden again took up his address: 'The inexorable arm of the King of Terrors has widowed every heart of sensibility. The chilling gloom of despair has frozen every soul. Cribb is glad. Carter rejoices. Hall, Cooper and Oliver are avenged.

England triumphs. Donnelly is dead and Erin is no more...'

One anonymous admirer published *A Monody on the Death of Dan Donnelly* in which he praised his idol's death-bed repentance for his sins. 'From the moment he found himself ill, he presaged death,' the pamphlet recorded. 'Therefore his clergy attended him every hour until he departed. So, thank Heaven, the last conflict was the best, when he fought against despair and the power of darkness, used the shield of faith and sought mercy from the captain of his salvation. What a happy circumstance if those sweet-tongued Christians who boast of their good works would only follow his example'.

Pierce Egan's favourite poetic tribute was the following, unsigned, which was published in *Carrick's Morning Post:*

> What dire misfortune has our land o'erspread,
> Our Irish champion's numbered with the dead;
> And he who never did to mortal bend
> By Death's cut short and Ireland's lost her Friend.
>
> Ah, cruel Death, why were you so unkind?
> To take Sir Dan and leave such trash behind
> As Gregson, Cooper, Carter, such a clan
> To leave behind and take so great a man.
>
> Oh, Erin's daughters, come and shed your tears
> On your Champion's grave, who loved you many years;
> To Erin's sons this day's a day of sorrow;
> Who have we now who will defend our Curragh?

Boxiana published the following brief lament from an anonymous Irishman:

> Mourn for our champion, snatched away
> From the fair Curragh's verdant ring;
> Mourn for his fist now wrapped in clay,
> No more the ponderous thump to fling.

Among the twenty pages of lamentations published by
Blackwood's Magazine were supposed tributes from scholars
in Greek, Hebrew and Latin. Language students may doubt
the seriousness of the writers and be amused at the licence
they took with, for instance, a Latin poem which read, in
part:

> Anglorum nunquam cohortem magnanimus in pugna tristi
> > Pugilum timuisti (heu ter legende DONNELLE)
> Sed si quis te val Hallus, vel Olivarius, in creparet,
> > Vel Cooperus (heu!! etc.)

Blackwood's also included a poem allegedly penned by
Lord Byron and sent from Venice. Entitled *Childe Daniel*
and following the style of Byron's celebrated *Childe Harold*,
it read thus:

> In Fancy-land there is a burst or two,
> > The spirits' tribute to the fallen, see
> On each scarr'd front the cloud of sorrow grow,
> > Bloating its sprightly shine. But what is he
> For whom grief's mighty butt is broached so free?
> Were his brows shadowed by the awful crown,
> > the Bishop's mitre, or high plumery
> Of the mailed warrior? Won he his renown
> On pulpit, throne or field, who Death hath now struck down?

> He won it in a field where arms are none,
> > Save those the mother gives to us.
> He was a climbing star which had not fully shown,
> > Yet promised in its glory to surpass
> > Our champion star ascendant, but alas;
> The sceptered shade that values earthly might
> And power, and pith, and bottom, as the grass,
> > Gave with his fleshless fist a buffet slight,
> Say, bottle-holding Leach, why ends so soon the fight?

What boots to inquire? Tis done, green mantled Erin
May weep, her hopes of milling sway pass by,
And Cribb, sublime, no lowlier rival fearing;
Repose, sole Ammon of the fistic sky,
Conceited, quaffing his blue ruin high,
Till comes the Swell, that comes to all men must,
By whose foul blows Sir Daniel low doth lie,
Summons the Champion to resign his trust
And mingles his with kings, slaves, chieftains, beggar's dust!

'Wordsworth' also contributed a poem to *Blackwood's*
which read, in part:

Yea, even I,
Albeit, who never 'ruffian'd' in the ring,
Nor know of 'challenge', save the echoing hills;
Nor 'fibbing' save that poesy doth feign;
Nor hear his fame, but as the mutterings
Of clouds contentious on Helvellyn's side,
Distant, yet deep, aguise a strange regret,
And mourn Donnelly — Honourable Sir Daniel:
(Blessings be on them, and eternal praise,
The Prince Regent and Dan Donnelly,
the Knighter and the Knighted); Love doth dwell
Here in these solitudes, and on corporal clay,
Doth for its season bear the self-same fire,
Impregnate with the same humanities,
Moulded and mixed, like others...

Blackwood's completed its trilogy of tributes allegedly contributed by Britain's foremost poets of the period with this piece by 'Sir Walter Scott':

SORROW IS DRY

A plaintive ballad

I

When to Peggie Baudie's daughter I first told Sir Daniel's death,
Like a glass of soda water, it took away her breath;
It took away your breath, my dear, and its sorely dimm'd your sight
And, aye, ye let the salt tear down fall for Erin's knight;
For he was a knight of glory bright, the spur ne'er deck'd a bolder,
Great George's blade itself was laid upon Sir Daniel's shoulder.

II

I took a turn along the street to breathe the Trongate air,
Carnegie's lass I chanced to meet with a bag of lemons fair;
Says I, 'Gude Meg, ohon! ohon! You've heard of Dan's disaster —
If I'm alive, I'll come at five and feed upon your master,
A glass or two no harm will do to either saint or sinner
And a bowl with friends will make amends for a so-so sort of dinner'.

III

I found Carnegie in his nook, upon the old settee
And dark and dismal was his look, as black as black might be;
Then suddenly the blood did fly and leave his face so pale
That scarce I knew, in altered hue, the bard of Largo's vale;
But Meg was winding up the jack, so off flew all my pains,
For large as cocks, two fat earocks I knew were hung in chains.

IV

Nevertheless, he did express his joy to see me there;
Meg laid the cloth and, nothing loth, I soon pull'd in my chair;
The mutton broth and bouilli broth came up in season due;
The Grace is said — when Provan's head at the door appears in view;
The bard at work like any Turk first nods an invitation,
For who so free as all the three from priggish botheration.

V

Ere long the Twaddies deck the board with a cod's head and shoulders
And the oyster sauce it surely was great joy to all beholders;
To George, our king, a jolly can of royal port is poured —
Our gracious kind who knighted Dan with his own shining sword;
The next we sip with trembling lip — 'tis of the claret clear —
To the hero dead that cup we shed and mix it with a tear.

VI

'Tis now your servant's turn to mix the nectar bowl;
Still on the king our thoughts we fix while round the goblets roll;
Great Jackson, Belcher, Scroggins, Gas, we celebrate in turns,
Each Christian, Jew and pagan, with the Fancy's flame that burns;
Carnegie's finger on the board a mimic circle draws
And, Egan-like, he expounds the rounds and pugilistic laws.

VII

'Tis thus that work heroic is suitably lamented—
Great Daniel's shade, I know it, dry grief had much resented;
What signify your tear and sigh? — A bumper is the thing,
Will gladden most the generous ghost of a champion of the king;
The tear and sigh, from voice and eye, must quickly pass away,
But the bumper good may be renewed until our dying day.

FINALE

Here rests his nob under the turf so green,
A milling cove — of Erin's pride and glory,
Sure such a hero gay ne'er was seen,
His fame transferr'd in future story.

Large was his morley and his pluck so fine;
In Ireland and England he did show it;
The lads he serv'd out with many a shine
When he had the office giv'n to 'Go it!'

But Dan is floor'd! He couldn't come to 'Time,'
No more to crack his joke and take his lunch;
His game's play'd out, although a trump so prime;
Death got the pull on him o'er whiskey punch!

Considerable scepticism has been levelled at the contention that the preceding poems were the works of Byron, Wordsworth and Scott. Richard M. Kain, in his book, *Dublin — in the age of William Butler Yeats and James Joyce*, claims that the elegiac verses on 'Sir Daniel' supplied to *Blackwood's* were 'fabricated' by William Maginn, a Cork-born humorous eccentric who was at one time editor of *Fraser's Magazine* and was a regular contributor to *Blackwood's*.

Support for the theory that the poems were 'fakes' might easily follow the realisation that the man who published them, the editor of *Blackwood's*, Professor John Wilson, or 'Christopher North', was notoriously over-imaginative. Certainly he let his pen run riot in recording his own 'memories' of Dan Donnelly.

Describing the late Irish champion as 'a warm and passionate admirer of the fine arts, particularly poetry and music, which often soothed his soul to melancholy,' Wilson maintained that Dan was 'deeply skilled in Oriental literature and is supposed by many to be the author of Anastasius, though he did not have the benefit of a regular education'.

Wilson, a noted athlete in his Oxford days who retained a strong interest in sport, especially boxing, really strayed into the realms of fiction when he contended that Donnelly was laid to rest, not in the Bully's Acre at Kilmainham, but in the vault of St. Patrick's Cathedral in Dublin. 'As the coffin was being laid into position,' he wrote, 'Mozart's celebrated Requiem was performed under the direction of Sir John Stevenson'.

Pierce Egan, whose *Boxiana* had been serialised by Wilson in *Blackwood's* along with the editor's praise for Egan as a boxing historian, admitted his ignorance of the meaning of many of the poetic tributes to Donnelly. 'We do not understand the gist of them,' said Egan, 'but no doubt they are truly interesting'. He regretted not having the assistance of Bob Gregson, the 'Poet Laureate of the Prize Ring' and he thought such pugilistic acquaintances as Bill Gibbons and Daniel Mendoza might possibly decipher the meaning of the Greek and Hebrew poems.

William Maginn

William Maginn, thought to be the man who actually penned the poetic tributes to the late Dan Donnelly allegedly written by Byron, Scott and Wordsworth and published in Blackwood's Magazine in May, 1820.

A humorous eccentric, Cork-born Maginn was a regular contributor to Blackwood's and later became editor of Fraser's Magazine.

Professor Wilson even provided his own suggested epitaph, which was rejected, for Donnelly's tombstone:

Underneath this pillar high
Lies Sir Dan Donnelly;
He was a stout and manly man
And people called him 'Buffing Dan'.
Knighthood he took from George's sword
And well he wore it, by my word;
He died at last, for 47
Tumblers of Punch he drank one even;
O'erthrown by Punch,
Unharmed by fist,
He died undefeated pugilist;
Such a buffer as Sir Dan
Ireland will never see again.

Many of the laments published by *Blackwood's* and other periodicals bemoaned the departed champion's love of liquor.

Morgan O'Doherty contributed the following to *Blackwood's:*

Majestic Donnelly, proud as thou art,
Like a cedar on top of Mount Hermon,
We lament that Death shamelessly made thee depart
In the gripes, like a blacksmith or chairman.

Oh, hadst thou been felled by Tom Cribb in the ring,
Or by Carter been milled to a jelly,
Oh, sure that would have been a more dignified thing
Than to kick for a pain in your belly.

A curse on the belly that robbed us of thee
And the bowels unfit for their office;
A curse on the poteen you swallowed too free,
For a stomach complaint, all the doctors agree,
Far worse than a headache or cough is.

Death who, like a cruel and insolent bully, drubs
All those he thinks fit to attack,
Cried 'Dan, my tight lad, try a touch of my mulligrubs,'
Which soon laid him flat on his back.

Thomas Jennings, a soda water manufacturer, of 7 Brown Street, Cork, wrote a sorrowful dirge which could be sung to the tune of *Molly Astore*. The words were as follows:

As down Exchequer Street I strayed a little time ago,
I chanced to meet an honest blade, his face brimful of woe;
I asked him why he seemed so sad, or why he sighed so sore;
Oh, Gramachree, och, Tom, says he, Sir Daniel is no more.

With that he took me straight away, and pensively we went
To where poor Dan's body lay in a wooden waistcoat pent,
And many a yard before we reached the threshold of his door,
We heard the keeners as they screeched, Sir Daniel is no more.

We entered soft, for feelings sad were stirring in our breast,
To take farewell of the lad who now had gone to rest;
We took a drop of Dan's poteen and joined the piteous roar;
Oh, where shall be his fellow seen, since Daniel is no more.

His was the fist whose mighty dint did Oliver defeat,
His was the fist that gave the hint it need not oft repeat,
His was the fist that overthrew his rivals o'er and o'er,
But now we cry, in pillalu, Sir Daniel is no more.

Cribb, Cooper, Carter, need not fear great Donnelly's renown,
For at his wake we're seated here while he is lying down,
For Death, the primest swell of all, has laid him on the floor
And left us here, alas, to bawl, Sir Daniel is no more.

EPITAPH

Here lies Sir Daniel Donnelly, a pugilist of fame;
In Ireland born and bred was he and he was genuinely game;
Then if an Irishman you be, when you have read this o'er,
Go home and drink the memory of him, who is no more.

Appraisals of the departed Irish champion generally found more merit in Donnelly's personality than in his prowess as a prizefighter. In the ring, though unbeaten in his brief career, his potential had not been realised. Obviously, a man who has not met his master must be accorded respect, but some of the English experts were not as convinced as their Irish counterparts that Dan's great strength and pride were enough to merit his ranking as the best heavyweight in the world.

Then, as today, nothing conclusive is to be gained by comparing the respective records, styles, scientific ability, punching power and resilience of Donnelly, Cribb, Spring, Carter and the other leading men of that period. Besides, favourites have a habit of falling now and again. Upsets are part and parcel of boxing and are a major cause of its continuing fascination. Who is to say which man merited top rating over his rivals?

Without a shadow of doubt, Donnelly and his contemporaries would be outclassed by the vastly superior

Professor John Wilson ('Christopher North'), the editor of Blackwood's Edinburgh Magazine, which carried no less than 20 pages of poetic lamentations in its May, 1820 edition on the death of Dan Donnelly.

Wilson offered his own epitaph for the departed Irish champion's tombstone, but it was not accepted.

technicians of today. The bare-knuckle breed would not have lasted more than a couple of one-sided rounds with the likes of Joe Louis, Rocky Marciano or Muhammad Ali.

But in his own time, Donnelly was at least as well equipped as any of the other claimants to the world heavy-weight championship. Whether he would have emerged victorious over each or any of his rivals for the title is, of course, merely a matter of conjecture.

Pierce Egan noted that Donnelly proved a disappointment to The Fancy in his only prizefight on English soil, against Tom Oliver. 'He did not look the same as against Cooper,' he wrote, 'but he was a most dangerous opponent from his great knowledge of throwing'.

Professor Wilson ('Christopher North') said the Irish champion 'seemed happy and contented with the fame he enjoyed under his native skies. It was never his desire to fight on this (English) side of the Channel. He was satisfied with being held as the most formidable buffer, as our good Irish friends denominate pugilists, among the potato-fed population of upwards of five million'.

'We have heard it said and are inclined to think it is true,' wrote Wilson in *Blackwood's,* 'that Sir Daniel's style of boxing showed, perhaps too strikingly, that he excelled at the miscellaneous fighting of Donnybrook Fair. He was not a straight or a quick hitter. The death of this illustrious man has left unsolved a problem. Could he have beaten Cribb? Could Carter have beaten him? Alas, vain interrogatories. The glory of Ireland is eclipsed — and ages may pass before another sun shines in what Mr. Egan so beautifully calls her pugilistic hemisphere'.

Commenting on 'the numberless tributes pouring in from all parts of the Empire,' Wilson recalled that Donnelly was 'a remarkably modest man who dreaded publicity. For ourselves, we will be satisfied with the destinies of Ireland should a Donnelly appear once in a thousand years'.

There was no doubting Dan's popularity with all sections of the community. The idol of the poor in his native land, he was widely accepted among those of the English aristocracy who followed boxing because of his warm personality, his good humour and his clear inclination to live up to the best image of the lovable Irish rogue.

T. G. Hazard, in a preface to his book *The Life of Dan Donnelly,* published just after the boxer's death, paid this warm tribute to his subject: 'He was brave, yet meek. He was wild, giddy and heedless of consequences, yet he was noble in his principles, compassionate and quiet. For since he first exhibited his courage it has not been known that he quarrelled with any person. He would rather bear the most severe injury than retaliate. Yet, if challenged by one who shed the smallest contempt on his country, he displayed the bravery which shall be handed down to posterity'.

Pierce Egan probably summed him up better than anyone. He wrote in *Boxiana:* 'Donnelly was a creature of the moment. He was excellent company, creating mirth and laughter all around him. His sayings were droll in the extreme and his behaviour was always decorous. He was generous, good natured and grateful. Tomorrow might, or might not, be provided for and it never created any uneasiness in his mind. He would say 'Devil may care'. He was an Irishman, every inch of him'.

I F YOU FOLLOW the road from Kilcullen, in County Kildare, for about two miles until you reach the Curragh, there you will find, on your left, Donnelly's Hollow. Down at its base you will see an eight foot tall limestone monument which commemorates Dan Donnelly's greatest ring triumph, over the Englishman George Cooper, at that very spot over a century and a half ago.

Only the summer picnickers and the grazing sheep occasionally disturb the peace of the scene which, on a cold December day in 1815, echoed to the ecstatic cheers of the Irish as their idol smashed the jaw of his gallant rival in a battle that lives on in story and song.

The memorial has, unfortunately, fallen victim to the ravages of time, the weather and vandals. But Donnelly's Hollow remains a favourite pilgrimage spot for followers of boxing, both natives and foreign visitors. School outings organisers often include it in their itineraries and the children take delight in walking in the famed fighter's footsteps.

The obelisk was erected in 1888, more than fifty years after Donnelly's death. Had it been left to his fellow countrymen, no permanent reminder of their departed hero would ever have been installed. It was an American heavyweight, Jake Kilrain, and an English boxer, Charley Mitchell, who got the idea after visiting the unmarked historic spot on October 18, 1887. Amazed that Donnelly, whose name was revered in boxing circles the world over, had been neglected in this way, Kilrain and Mitchell, who both boasted of Irish blood in their veins, suggested a fund to raise by public subscriptions the cost of having a suitable monument erected.

The great John L. Sullivan, then heavyweight champion of the world, who was on an exhibition tour of Ireland and Britain along with Kilrain and Mitchell, was one of the first to contribute to the fund. Sullivan, both of whose parents were Irish-born, had himself been inspired by the stirring tales of Dan Donnelly when he set out on the path to ring fame.

Sufficient cash was gathered, the Irish rather shamefacedly matching the generous donations from abroad, to enable the

John L. Sullivan, last of the great bare-fist champions of the world, who was one of the subscribers to the fund for the monument to Dan Donnelly on the Curragh of Kildare.

Sullivan, 'the Boston Strong Boy', came from hardy Irish stock. His father was born in Tralee, Co. Kerry, and his mother was an emigrant from Athlone, Co. Roscommon.

fund's treasurer, Mr. Richard Kavanagh, to order the memorial. The work was entrusted to Mr. Peter Hynes of Messrs. Farrell and Son, Glasnevin, Dublin, and the obelisk was completed 'in a most artistic and satisfactory manner'.

On the front face of the monument the following inscription appeared in raised letters:

DONNELLY BEAT COOPER ON THIS SPOT,

13th DEC. 1815

Below this, on two separate shields, appeared:

Dan Donnelly	George Cooper
Born in Dublin, 1770	Born in Staffordshire, 1791
Died 1820	Died 1834

On the left hand side:

Donnelly fought Tom Hall, Tom Oliver

On the right hand side:

Cooper fought Lancaster, Joy, Molineaux,
Robinson, Kendrick.

On back of memorial:

Erected by public subscription 1888.

If the date of Donnelly's birth as given on the original inscription was factual, he was fifty years old when he died. This is surely way off the mark. He was hardly twenty-one years older than his opponent, Cooper, as this would suggest!

As with the handsome tombstone that once marked the champion's grave at Kilmainham, the Curragh monument proved none too popular with British soldiers based on the nearby military camp. It was a frequent target for stones and other missiles. Fortunately the obelisk proved as indestructible under attack as did Donnelly himself in the ring.

It was not until the 1950s that real interest in the historic spot was revived, coinciding with the acquisition by Kilcullen publican James J. Byrne Jnr. of Donnelly's arm. A Donnelly Monument Renovation Committee was formed, under the chairmanship of Mr. P. Brady, and an appeal was launched for funds to pay for the cleaning-up of the Hollow and the placing of a plaque at the foot of the monument. Response to the appeal was generous.

The plaque, I am happy to note, ignored the earlier inscribed date of Donnelly's birth and gave the generally-accepted date. The new inscription reads:

'Dan Donnelly, Champion of Ireland. Born in Dublin, 1788. Occupation, carpenter. Began ring career by beating Tom Hall at the Curragh, Sept. 1814. Hall left the ring in 14th round crying 'Foul'. In December 1815, Donnelly beat George Cooper at the Curragh. Three years later he went to England and challenged all-comers. In a 34-round fight, he beat Tom Oliver with a heavy blow on the ear followed by a cross buttock.'

The renovation job was completed in 1953, the year of An Tostal. In keeping with the countrywide festival events, Kilcullen Tostal Committee showed commendable enterprise in organising a 're-match' between Donnelly and Cooper!

'Dan Donnelly Fights Again' read the astonishing front page headline in the *Leinster Leader*. The story told of thousands of excited spectators cramming into Donnelly's Hollow on the previous Sunday afternoon, April 19, 1953, to witness the 'fight'. If those who paid one to five shillings (5p to 25p) to stand or sit on the historic slopes let their imagination run freely, they might have convinced themselves they were watching the real thing instead of a re-enactment of the famous contest.

The crowd quickly got into the spirit of the occasion and cheered almost as heartily as did their predecessors back in 1815 as 'Donnelly' (played by local amateur boxer Jim Berney) surged into the attack against 'Cooper' (Irish Army Sergeant Kevin McCourt). To add authenticity to the scene, members of a Gaelic football club dressed in period costume sat around the ringside cheering on 'the Irish champion'.

True to history, 'Miss Kelly' (C. Whelan) climbed through the ropes and pleaded with 'Dan' to win as she had placed her entire fortune in bets on his victory. She was 'rescued' from the ring by her father, 'Capt. Kelly' (played by Gerry Kelly).

It was all good, clean fun and the spectators took delight in joining in, even though some got a little over-enthusiastic. One of the participant's seconds was led away from the scene nursing a sore head after getting in the way of a swinging shillelagh.

It was only revealed afterwards that the 'fight' almost had to be postponed because, in a realistic rehearsal a week beforehand, Kevin McCourt su ffered damaged ribs. He recovered sufficiently as to go through with it, much to the relief of the organisers.

So successful was the 1953 pageant at the Curragh that it was decided to repeat it the following year. So once again, on May 16, 1954, 'Donnelly and Cooper' squared off. The crowd who had come to see a mixture of action, thrills and farce were not disappointed. Even the notoriously inadequate Broughton Rules which governed bare-knuckle fighting were blatantly ignored and the affair ended up in a good-humoured 'free-for-all' involving boxers, seconds and spectators.

There are several other existing reminders of the renowned Irish champion, apart from the Curragh memorial and the mummified arm in The Hideout at Kilcullen. Another tavern, in Naas, County Kildare, has adopted the name 'Donnelly's Hollow', although it is quite a distance from the Curragh. It has a 'Dan Donnelly Bar' and a lounge stained-glass window depicting the monument in Donnelly's Hollow.

At the entrance to an estate at Johnswell, County

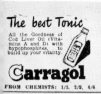
The Irish Press

Do Cum Slóipe Dé agus Onópa na héipeann

The Truth in the News.

Vol. XXIII, No. 93.   MONDAY, APRIL 20, 1953.   PRICE 2d.

LD-TIME FIST BATTLE COMES ALIVE AGAIN IN FAMED DONNELLY'S HOLLOW

Korean Peace Talk: Begin Next Saturd

First Pri Exchar

(REUTER, UNITED PRE

PA

FULL-SCALE Korean armistic
next Saturday, U.N. and Com
to-day. At this brief meeting, t
dropped their demand that all pr
gardless of their wishes—the
previous talks.

The exchange of United Nat
and wounded prisoners of war be

Twelve British, 30 Ameri-
cans, four Turks, and one each
from the fighting forces of
Canada, South Africa, the
Philippines and Greece will be
released in the exchange, to
be made in two stages.

A Columbia broadcasting System broadcast identified the first
American disabled captive to be
returned as Carl Kirchenhausen
of New York city. First British
prisoner to be exchanged was
trooper E. O'Donnell with an
address at St. Helen's, Lancashire.

A brisk fight was raging
about a mile to the west as the
Communist ambulances rolled into
the neutral zone. The Allied
convoy entered it from the south
some minutes later.

The Communist New China
news agency reported yesterday
that the fourth group of United
Nations sick and wounded prisoners were expected to arrive at
Kaesong from Pyonking to-mor-
row for their return to the Allies.

Prisoner Murdered

Communists released by the

 me of the large crowd
ho went to Donnelly's
ollow, Kilcullen, Co.
ldare, to watch the re-
acted prize fight be-
een Donnelly and
ooper (Report and
other picture—Page 7).

The 'Light' Is Out On O'Connell Bridge

The Irish Press report of the pageant staged in Donnelly's Hollow in April 1953, when a re-enactment of Donnelly's fight with Cooper was staged.

Kilkenny, the huge iron gates are supported by stone replicas of a pair of fists. These are said to have been modelled on the fists of Dan Donnelly. The house was once owned by members of the Kelly family (Capt. William Kelly being the man who 'discovered' Donnelly) so this would add credence to the belief.

Quite recently, I came across two fascinating mementoes of the celebrated Irish boxing champion of the last century. His five-gallon whiskey measure and his pipe are in the possession of Mr. Henry B. Fottrell, the retired head of a well-known Dublin firm of solicitors, at his home in Castle-knock, County Dublin.

The huge copper spirit measure has a small plaque attached which is inscribed 'Sir Dan Donnelly, Irish champion, Pill Lane, 1820'. This is evidence that Dan himself took his 'knighthood' seriously enough to have it recorded on at least one display item in the last of his four Dublin public houses.

The interesting history of the copper jug is recorded in a letter sent to Mr. Fottrell by the auctioneer who sold it to him in 1940. The letter reads as follows:

August 22, 1940

Dear Mr. Fottrell,

This old five-gallon copper measure belonged originally to Sir Daniel Donnelly, Irish boxing champion, Dublin. It was used by him in his 'lushing crib' (punch house) in Pill Lane. At the sale of Donnelly's effects in February 1820, it was purchased by Hugh Blaney, 14 Lower Exchange Street and Smock Alley, where it was a showpiece until Blaney's death on August 22nd, 1885, aged 95 years. My father, Michael Butler, of 29 Upper Liffey Street and 26, 126, 127, 128 Upper Abbey Street, bought it at Blaney's sale in 1885. Patrick Cooke, auctioneer, Upper Abbey Street, had this sale. Peter Maher, Irish champion, recently deceased, who lived with Dan Murphy in one of my father's cottages in Farrell's Court, off Upper Abbey Street (now the back entrance to Jervis Street Hospital) used try to lift it full with one arm, as Donnelly was reputed to have done frequently.

John Butler,
29 Lower Ormond Quay,
Dublin.

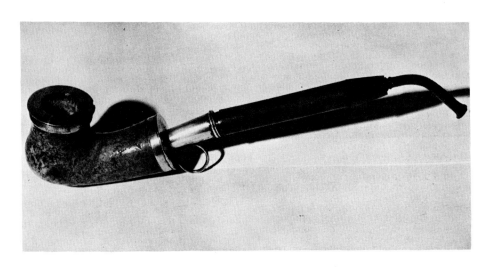

Above — A Silver-mounted pipe presented to Dan Donnelly by his patron, Captain William Kelly, after the Irish champion's victory over George Cooper at the Curragh. Around the rim is the inscription 'Dan'l Donnelly, 13th Dec. 1815' and a small silver plate at the base bears the initials 'D.D.' — The pipe is almost a foot long.

Right — A five-gallon whiskey measure used by Dan Donnelly at the last of his four Dublin pubs. Made of copper, it has an inscribed plaque which reads 'Sir Dan Donnelly, Irish Champion, Pill Lane, 1820'. Donnelly, it was claimed, could lift the jug, full of spirits with one arm — a feat that another Irish champion, Peter Maher, could not match.

The pipe was also sold to Mr. Fottrell by the same auctioneer in 1941. The handsome, silver-mounted pipe, almost a foot long, was presented to Donnelly by his patron, Capt. Kelly, after his triumph over George Cooper at the Curragh. Around the rim is the inscription 'Dan'l Donnelly, 13th Dec. 1815' and a small silver plate at the base bears the initials 'D.D.'. The story of the pipe was told in a letter from its previous owner to the auctioneer, Mr. Butler.

May 21, 1941

Dear Mr. Butler,

All I know of Dan Donnelly's pipe was told me by my mother, who gave it to me with some other oddments. It was after one of Donnelly's fights that souvenir hunters got busy and he distributed odd pieces. His pipe was the last thing left and my father begged so hard he handed it to him for a keepsake. It has been in our possession ever since. I cannot tell you the year but my father is dead now over 60 years.

Miss K. Tierney,
80a Vernon Avenue,
Clontarf,
Dublin.

Strangely, and sadly, there is no permanent reminder of Donnelly in his native city. Dubliners stand guilty of neglecting one of their earliest and greatest fighting sons. They have left it to 'outsiders' to perpetuate his memory. Admittedly, it is impossible to locate the exact spot of his birthplace in Townsend Street and there must remain an element of doubt as to the precise location of his now-unmarked grave in the Bully's Acre at Kilmainham. Might not the city fathers or the tourism chiefs see fit to erect a plaque on the wall of the newly-erected office block at the corner of Chancery Street (formerly Pill Lane) and Greek Street, where Dan had the last of his four Dublin public houses and where he died on February 18, 1820. Lesser men have been honoured in this way.

HALL OF FAME

Dan Donnelly's contribution to the long and colourful history of boxing was duly recognised in 1960, when the American magazine *The Ring* elected the celebrated Irish champion to its 'Boxing Hall of Fame'.

The Hall of Fame, instituted in 1954, consists of three groups. The Pioneer Group, to which Donnelly was admitted, is for those who were active in the days of bare-fist boxing and who did much to establish boxing as a world sport. The Old-Timers Group is for gloved boxers who campaigned before 1919, and the Modern Group is made up of ringsters who were active after 1919 and who have been retired at least two years before being considered for the Hall of Fame.

Boxers who are honoured by being admitted to the Hall of Fame are elected by a special committee of writers, broadcasters and directors of the Hall of Fame under the chairmanship of the editor of *The Ring*.

Donnelly was the only pugilist chosen to join the Pioneer group in 1960 and he was the first Irishman to be included in that section since the Hall of Fame's inauguration year, when three Irish-born boxers, John Morrissey, Jack McAuliffe and Nonpariel Jack Dempsey (not the famed world heavyweight champion, but a middleweight from County Kildare whose real name was John Kelly) were so honoured.

Immediately after *The Ring* announcement that it had elected Donnelly to its Hall of Fame, there was a great re-awakening of interest in the legendary barefist champion of Ireland. Dan Parker, sports editor of the *New York Mirror,* was flooded with letters asking about Donnelly and his severed arm.

Around the early 1960s, too, the name of Donnelly once again threatened to make boxing headlines. Jackie Donnelly, a hard-punching lightweight from Buffalo, New York, who claimed to be a direct descendant of the Irish champion, caused quite a stir of excitement by going undefeated in an amateur career of twenty-five fights. This included several

Golden Gloves championship wins.

Jackie turned professional in 1958 and, over the next few years, beat respected fighters like Orlando Zulueta, Tommy Tibbs, Chico Velez and Italy's Paolo Rosi. But he failed to fulfil his early promise and faded from the scene without ever getting in range of a world title opportunity. Today it is his illustrious ancestor, not Jackie, who keeps the name of Donnelly alive in the hearts of fight fans the world over.

Dan Donnelly enters the Hall of Fame

U.S. HONOUR GREAT DUBLINER OF LAST CENTURY

THE 19th century Irish heavyweight, Dan Donnelly of Dublin, has been named to the Ring magazine's Hall of Fame in New York—the highest honour that can be bestowed on an outstanding sportsman. He is one of six old-time boxing greats selected, including former world heavyweight champion Tommy Burns, Welsh lightweight Freddie Welsh, and Joe Choynski, the great U.S. heavyweight who three times fought Gentleman Jim Corbett.

The 1960 selections bring to 61 the number of fighters named to the honour by writers, broadcasters, an Old Timers Committee and directors of the Hall of Fame set up by Ring's editor, Nat Fleischer.

The new members are:—

DAN DONNELLY, the Dubliner who was the first British heavyweight champion of Irish extraction. He gained the British championship by beating George Cooper in 11 rounds in 1814 and beat Tom Oliver in 34 rounds in 1819, when more than half a million dollars was wagered on the bout.

JOE CHOYNSKI, the first American heavyweight of Jewish extraction to win distinction. He fought Jim Corbett three times, the first ending in a "no contest" and Corbett taking the other two. He reached a peak by boxing Jim Jeffries to a draw in 1897.

TOMMY BURNS (Canada) who defeated Marvin Hart in 20 rounds in 1906 to stamp himself a claimant for the title and then won universal recognition in 1907 by beating Jack O'Brien. He lost the title to Jack Johnson in Sydney Australia, in 1908.

JOHNNY KILBANE of the U.S., who held the featherweight title from 1912 when he won it

from Abe Attell until 1923 when he lost it to Eugene Criqui.

FREDDY WELSH, of Pontypridd, South Wales, one of the classiest defensive boxers of all time who held the lightweight title from 1914 until May 1917 when he lost to Benny Leonard.

JACK BRITTON of the U.S., a defensive artist who defeated Ted Kid Lewis for the welterweight title in 1919 and held it until Mickey Walker took it from him in November, 1922.

Long arms

Donnelly, who was at the height of his fame and popularity in the early 1800's, had arms so long that he could fasten his knee breeches at the knee without stooping.

Born in Townsend Street, Dublin, in 1786. Dan first practised the Noble Art as an amateur. He was, however, prevailed upon by a racehorse owner, Capt. Kelly, of the Curragh, to take to the ring professionally.

In December, 1815, he was matched with that great English fighter, George Cooper. The fight took place near Kilcullen before a crowd estimated at 20,000 and Donnelly won the fight, breaking his opponent's jaw in the 11th round.

Knighted

A successful career followed in the English ring, and it is related that after one of his many victories, he was knighted in a tavern near Crawley Commons by the then Prince Regent.

Dublin vintners seem to have held Sir Dan in particularly high esteem, for they presented him with no fewer than four public houses. Unfortunately, Sir Dan,

it seems, was his own best customer.

He died penniless in 1820 at the age of thirty-four, and he was buried in the Bully's Acre now Kilmainham.

Grave robbed

On the very night of the interment, the grave was robbed by a medical student. Following police intervention he was made re-bury the body, but first he amputated the right arm.

The arm later was brought to Scotland, then to Belfast, and is now in the "Hide Out," Kilcullen, two miles from the scene of his most spectacular triumph.

Evening Herald,
December 6, 1960

BIBLIOGRAPHY

The following is a list of the principal published sources which yielded useful information during the compilation of this book. Due to the absence of a prior guide to specific data on the life of Dan Donnelly, the search for relevant material proved laborious but it had its many moments of recompense when something would turn up, often in the most unexpected publications. The list is by no means a complete one, but it does provide a guide to the main sources and dates.

BOOKS

Anonymous, *A Monody on the Death of Daniel Donnelly*, Dublin 1820.

Ball, James Moores, *The Sack-'Em-Up Men: an account of the rise and fall of the modern resurrectionists*, Edinburgh and London, 1928.

Batchelor, Denzil, *The Boxing Companion*, London 1964.

Brady, James, *Strange Encounters: tales of famous fights and famous fighters*, London 1946

Bryant, Arthur, *The Age of Elegance 1812-1822*, London 1950.

Buchanan-Taylor, W., assisted by James Butler, *What Do You Know About Boxing?* London 1947.

Chart, D.A., *The Story of Dublin*, Dublin 1932.

Crean, Rev. Cyril F., editor, *Parish of the Sacred Heart, Donnybrook*, Dublin 1966.

D'Alton, John, *The History of County Dublin*, Dublin 1838.

Edmundson, Joseph, *Great Moments in Boxing*, London 1974.

Egan, Pierce, *Boxiana (Vols. 2-4)*, London 1818, 1821, 1828.

Fitzpatrick, William J., *History of the Dublin Catholic Cemeteries*, Dublin 1900.

Fleischer, Nat, *The Ring Record Book and Boxing Encyclopedia*, New York 1962.

Ford, John, *Prizefighting: the age of Regency boximania*, Devon 1971.

Hazard, T.G., *The Life of Dan Donnelly, late champion of Ireland*, Dublin 1820.

Healy, James N., *The Mercier Book of Old Irish Street Ballads, Vol. 3, The Irish at Play*, Cork 1969.

Hibbert, Christopher, *George IV, Prince of Wales*, London 1972.

Hibbert, Christopher, *George IV, Regent and King 1811-1830*, London 1973.

Hyde, Douglas, *Songs and Poems of Raftery*, Dublin 1933.

Joyce, Weston St. John, *The Neighbourhood of Dublin*, Dublin and Waterford 1912.

Kain, Richard M., *Dublin in the Age of William Butler Yeats and James Joyce*, Oklahoma 1962.

Little, Dr. George A., *Malachi Horan Remembers*, Dublin 1943.

Lynch, Bohun, *The Prize Ring*, London 1925.

MacThomais, Eamonn, *Me Jewel and Darlin' Dublin*, Dublin 1974.

Maxwell, Constanta, *Dublin Under the Georges 1714-1830*, London 1936.

McCall, P. J., *In the Shadow of St. Patrick's* (first read as a paper before the Irish National Literary Society on April 27, 1893), Dublin 1894.

Miles, Henry Downes, *Pugilistica: the history of British boxing* (Vols. 1–3), Edinburgh 1880-1906.

O Lochlainn, Colm, *Irish Street Ballads*, Dublin 1939.

O'Neill, Capt. Francis, *Irish Minstrels and Musicians*, Chicago 1913.

Phillips Browne, Noel, *The Horse in Ireland*, London 1967.

Prestidge, Dennis, *Tom Cribb at Thistleton Gap*, Leicestershire 1971.

Priestley, J.B., *The Prince of Pleasure and his Regency 1811-1820*, London 1969.

Shepherd, T. B., compiler, *The Noble Art: an anthology*, London 1950.

Wignall, Trevor, *Prides of the Fancy*, London 1928.

NEWSPAPERS AND PERIODICALS

Blackwood's Magazine, March and May, 1820.

Boxing Illustrated, February 1964.

Carberry's Annual, Christmas 1950.

Carrick's Morning Post, Sept. 16, 22, 24, 1814; Feb. 19, 23, 1820.

Dublin Evening Post, Feb. 22, 1820.

Dublin Journal, Sept. 18, 20, 1819; March 1, 1820.

Dublin Penny Journal, Aug. 25, 1832; Nov. 16, 1833.

Evening Herald, May 31, 1941; May 1, 7, 12, 13, 1965; March 16, 1968; Sept. 5, 1970; Jan. 29, 1972.

Freeman's Journal, Feb. 19 and March 4, 1820.

Irish Book Lover, Vol. XXVIII, Feb. 1942.

Irish Independent, April 20, 1953; March 3, 1961; June 17, 1966.

Irish Journal of Medical Science, Feb. 1929.

Irish Press, April 20, 1953.

Kildare Archaeological Society Journal, Vol. III, 1899-1902.

Leinster Leader, April 25, 1953; May 16, 1954.

Nationalist and Leinster Times, April 18 and 25, 1953.

Saunders' Newsletter, Feb. 19, 1820.

Sporting Magazine, Nov., Dec. 1815; June 1817; March 1820.

Sunday Independent, April 19, 1953.

Sunday Press, March 24, 1974.

Tuam Herald, Sept. 27, 1930; Oct. 24, 1931.

The Ring, Jan and Sept., 1961.

PROGRAMME

Donnelly's Hollow Pageant 1954.

MANUSCRIPT

Kelly, Capt. William, manuscript number 13,562 in National Library of Ireland.

Index

Publications and song titles in italic